EMPIRE OF THE SONG

VICTORIAN
SONGS & MUSIC

Olivia Bailey

Published in 2002 by Caxton Editions
20 Bloomsbury Street
London WC1B 3JH
a member of the Caxton Publishing Group

© 2002 Caxton Publishing Group

Designed and produced for Caxton Editions
by Open Door Limited
Langham, Rutland
Editing: Mary Morton
Setting: Jane Booth
Colour Separation: GA Graphics, Stamford, UK

Title: Empire of the Song, Victorian Songs & Music
ISBN: 1 84067 468 7

EMPIRE OF THE SONG

VICTORIAN
SONGS & MUSIC

Olivia Bailey

CAXTON EDITIONS

Preface

Queen Victoria reigned from 1837 to 1901 and this book covers the development of popular music over those 64 years which saw some of the greatest changes in music that Britain had ever seen. It was the height of the British Empire which meant many cross-cultural influences were involved as well as it being a time of great social change. From the polkas and waltzes which characterised the beginning of her reign, the reintroduction of Christmas carols through the influence of her German husband Prince Albert, the start of music hall in the 1850s and the operettas of Gilbert and Sullivan, through to the invention of the gramophone in 1877, Victorian Britain was most definitely the Empire of the Song.

Some men see things as they are and ask why.
Others dream things that never were and ask why not.

George Bernard Shaw (1856–1950)

Above: Victorian London.

Contents

Introduction

> *"The modern popular song reminds one of the outer circumference of our terribly overgrown towns. It is for the people who live in those unhealthy regions, people who have the most false ideals, who are always scrambling for subsistence, who think that the commonest rowdyism is the highest expression of human emotion; for them, this popular music is made, and it is made with a commercial object, of snippets, of slang"*
>
> *Sir Charles Hubert Parry (1848–1918)*

Queen Victoria came to the throne in 1837. Her reign, spanning over 60 years, saw some of the most amazing social changes Great Britain had ever seen. She became the figurehead of a vast Empire and was the source of the nation's inspiration.

The Victorians firmly believed in the strength of their Empire and its global influence. The generation before had defeated Napoleon Bonaparte, leaving England free to pursue its industrial revolution and all that that entailed. They believed that God was on their side for they worked hard, had strict morals and applied their religious fervour to the sciences and industry.

The Victorians were vigorous and enthusiastic about life and as a nation were extraordinarily industrious. They wrote huge tomes and novels, travelled across continents, encountering new "savage" cultures, established trade, invented hundreds of machines including the bicycle, and pushed forward the boundaries of science. Cloth, pharmaceuticals and steel all poured out of the factories; the railways spread their iron tracks across the countryside. In amongst all the hard work and the sound of the factories could be heard the music. Victorian music had to be popular to survive, although this did not hinder great diversity in the forms it took. The laws of supply and demand operated relentlessly and the weak fell by the wayside. Unlike today, ballet and opera paid their way without any form of subsidy and it was the music hall, not the theatre, that made them popular. The music halls were the epitome of mass culture. In their early days music halls had a policy of giving the masses not what they wanted but what the management thought they ought to have, although this changed as the years passed.

Classical music was brought to the masses through promenade concerts, complete with gimmicks in much the same way that we today go to open air concerts of classical music and expect to see fireworks and laser shows. However, there was a paradox in Victorian music. It was the time of both the large choir and the small piano. The most prominent feature of Victorian music was that it was not compartmentalised. The audience could go in one evening from a ballad concert to a promenade concert, on to a music hall and then back to a musical evening at home.

The amount of music written and performed in Victorian England was enormous. Week after week dozens of drawing-room ballads rolled off the publishers' printing presses. Towards the close of the century popular songs were recorded within a few days of their first performance. Music was everywhere. There were barrel organs and barrel pianos in the streets, churning out their raucous tunes, German "oompah" bands at every turn and military bands playing on bandstands in the parks. Almost every house had someone practising their scales on the newly invented upright piano. In fact, it is actually difficult to say which was the most powerful force in Victorian music – the music hall or the piano. However, London was short on classical concerts, chamber music and formal piano recitals.

The quality of Victorian popular music varied greatly. The best is exemplified by the comic operas of Gilbert and Sullivan. Music hall songs, like modern pop songs, were catchy but predictable. The Victorians were sentimental and aesthetically conservative but they were also sharp, knowledgeable, cynical and eclectic, being able to mix music hall ditties with Beethoven's Fifth Symphony played by four brass bands, for instance.

Above: it was the music hall, not the theatre, that made opera and ballet popular.

Queen Victoria

Queen Victoria was born on 24 May 1819, the only child of Edward, Duke of Kent, and his wife, Victoria Maria Louisa of Saxe-Coburg. In 1837 she succeeded her uncle, William IV and three years later she married her first cousin, Albert of Saxe-Coburg Gotha. Together they had nine children.

When she first came to the throne, the country's morale was low but she overcame the nation's cynicism toward the monarchy with her down-to-earth leadership and high moral code. She was politically active through her relationship with the prime minister Lord Melbourne and also through her husband's influence. Although Albert was unpopular with the general public at first, he eventually won favour through his vision of the Great Exhibition of 1851 and was given the title Prince Consort. Albert was also extremely interested in the arts and sciences in general and this filtered through to the entire nation. Queen Victoria and her family loved both music and dancing, and she was a role model to her people in this respect.

The most notable achievements of their reign was the expansion of the British Empire, which doubled in size, and the implementation of a constitutional monarchy, both of which affected all walks of life in Great Britain.

Sadly Prince Albert died of typhoid in 1861 and Victoria never recovered from her loss. She remained in mourning for the rest of her life and the nation mourned with her. Indeed, the music became more sombre to reflect this.

Queen Victoria died on 22 January 1901, but her influence continues to this day.

> *The writer who possesses the creative gift owns something of which he is not always master – something that at time strangely wills and works for itself.*
>
> *Charlotte Brontë (1816–55)*

Above: Queen Victoria as a child.

8

9

*Above: Queen Victoria and Prince Albert
and their young family.*

Dances of the Empire

The passion for dancing during the Victorian era cut across all social levels and a wide variety of new dances were introduced. These dances were of the type that we know today as old-time dances and even in the casinos and saloons of the working classes, couples danced hectic figures of quadrilles and polkas. The main difference was that in the saloons and casinos the men kept their hats on but at the balls and country dances of the upper classes they took them off.

The young Queen Victoria was very fond of dancing. She was a high-spirited girl with all the appetites of her German ancestry and she looked good on the dance floor and she knew it. She was the last person to cut herself off from innocent pleasures because of protocol although there was still a body of opinion in the upper classes that considered the waltz indecent because it involved physical contact between the dance partners. When Victoria came to the throne in 1837 the waltz was in the process of being accepted by high society. It had been more or less respectable since about 1812, the year it was introduced at the exclusive Almack's Assembly Rooms, King Street, St James's and it was welcomed because it was a "closed" dance, that is there were no changes of partner. It was, therefore, the first modern dance in which dance as a social phenomenon took precedence over dance as a means of interacting with a member of the opposite sex.

Above: Queen Victorias costume ball at Buckingham Palace in 1845.

In 1844, the polka made its appearance in London having done the rounds in Paris. Like the waltz, the polka was a closed dance and evidence of its popularity was soon apparent. At a ball given by the Duke of Wellington in honour of Queen Victoria's birthday, the polka was danced six times during the course of the evening. At this time, the established programme of dancing at a ball was quadrille, waltz, quadrille, polka or other dance, quadrille, waltz, quadrille, polka or other dance.

In 1845 five o'clock tea dances were introduced. They were described by the magazine *Punch* as "the nearest approach to which seems to have been the capers cut by a bull among the cups and saucers in a china shop". The appeal of the polka at tea dances was so widespread that its form was simplified and it remained popular throughout the century. Although the waltz and the polka challenged the quadrille, which had been introduced in 1815, the old styles of dancing also received a boost from the general revival of dancing. In 1817 the lancers, a variant of the quadrille, was born but it was not danced in respectable circles until 1850. Originally the dance called the lancers was done to just one tune, namely 'The Lancers', but it became so popular that people began to dance it to other tunes. The lancers eventually eclipsed the quadrille, except at court balls and dance assemblies. Because of the effect upon the public that the polka had had, there were attempts to introduce other European modes of dance such as the mazurka and the polonaise. The cotillon also received support at fashionable balls. It was a grown-up version of musical chairs and so was popular at the end of the evening, when feet and ankles were tired.

11

State Balls

A typical state ball in the 1840s would open with a set of quadrilles, followed by waltzes. Then there would be a break while the Queen rested, during which the band would play a quadrille or two as background music. Then there would be more dancing of quadrilles, waltzes and a couple of polkas until supper was taken at midnight. After supper, the guests had to endure, or enjoy, a session of bagpipe music before they danced to another group of quadrilles or waltzes and the ball ended about two o'clock in the morning.

The state balls at Buckingham Palace clearly showed that these were occasions for social one-upmanship rather than just simple pleasure. The ladies wore full evening dress and the men wore uniform or full court dress which was dresscoat, breeches and silk stockings and buckles. If the military guest in uniform went with his sword then he would be etiquette-bound to wear it all evening.

Above: Queen Victorias Georgian costume ball at Buckingham Palace.

This was kept up throughout Victoria's reign, the Prince of Wales continuing the tradition when the Queen became too old. After the death of Prince Albert enthusiasm for dancing had waned a little in deference to the Queen's mourning. This decline in the popularity of dancing was warmly greeted by the upper classes and aristocracy who had been obliged by social etiquette to attend so many balls and dances.

The aristocracy were renowned for having two left feet. Those who really liked dancing contented themselves with home balls which continued to be given by members of the upper classes who were living on a tight budget. They were glad that the giving of great balls was no longer required of them as it could be an expensive business.

Grand Balls

A typical grand ball was given by the Marchioness of Salisbury at Hatfield House in 1895. There were 700 guests and two large bands. Women were expected to use these grand balls as a means of fashionable display and, if unmarried, to find a suitable husband. The etiquette of a fashionable ball was all important. A hostess giving a ball in London who gave out programmes was quickly dismissed by her guests as being lacking in sophistication. Programmes were fine for country balls but not for London. A hostess who expected guests to bring their invitation cards with them was also in trouble as guests should only do this for a masked ball. In fact, the word "ball" was never used on invitation cards for these functions. An ordinary at-home card was used with "Dancing" printed in the corner and invitations were made out by the lady of the house, never the husband.

The key figure in Victorian dancing was the dancing master or mistress who acted as master of ceremonies as well as dance teacher. They took their work as seriously as they took themselves and had a reputation for being particularly pompous. Their jargon exemplifies this. There was a Mister Tenniel of London who announced to the "Nobility, Gentry and his friends" that his course of instruction included "dancing, deportment and modified Calisthenics, with his Systolic and Dyastolic Staff". At state balls the dancing master was a privileged outsider, there to organise discreetly the frequently complex manoeuvres. All grand people sent their children to dancing masters; even older men did not avoid the dancing master.

After the Ball is Over

A little maiden climbed an old man's knee,

Begged for a story, "Do, Uncle, Please.

Why are you lonely, why do you roam?

Have you no sweetheart, have you no home?"

"I had a sweetheart, long, long ago

Why we were not wed, you soon

shall know. List to my story, I'll tell it all.

I broke her heart, pet, after the ball."

Her eyes were shining, in the big ballroom,

Softly the organ was playing a tune.

There stood my sweetheart, my love, my own.

Wishing some water, I left the room.

When I returned, pet, there stood a man

Kissing my sweetheart, as lovers can.

Down went the glass, pet, broke in the fall,

Just as my heart was, after the ball.

After the ball is over,
just at the break of dawn,

After the dance is ended,
and all the stars are gone.

Many the heart that's aching,
if you could read them all.

Many the fond hope that's vanished,
after the ball.

After the ball is over,
just at the break of dawn,

After the dance is ended,
and all the stars are gone.

Many the heart that's aching,
if you could read them all.

Many the fond hope that's vanished,
after the ball.

After the ball is over,
just at the break of dawn,

After the dance is ended,
and all the stars are gone.

Many the heart that's aching,
if you could read them all.

Many the fond hope that's vanished,
after the ball.

Many years have gone by; I have not wed –

True to my sweetheart, though she is dead.

She tried to tell me, tried to explain.

I would not listen, pleading in vain.

One day a letter came from this man.

He was her brother, the letter ran.

That's why I'm lonely, no home at all –

I broke her heart, pet, after the ball.

The Dance Saloons

The dance saloons of the West End, by contrast, were patronised by a wide variety of men and women, despite their reputations as dens of debauchery. Some of the more respectable were run by dancing masters whose students, mainly young women, would bring their friends both male and female at so much per head with refreshments and supper included. These young women belonged to the lower middle classes. Other dancing places did deserve their low reputations. Situated in or near the Haymarket, the centre of night life in London,

were the Argyll Rooms on the site of the present Criterion Theatre where brawls were commonplace. The Argyll Rooms catered for the smartest men about town and also the cream of London courtesans. In between dances the ladies could partake of the favourite drinks of this period such as brandy and soda or sherry and seltzer.

The better class of men only went there on Saturdays. To preserve the image of the Argyll, capable dancers of both sexes were admitted free, just like in today's top night-

Above: masked courtesans of the dance saloons.

clubs, and the place was regularly visited by the police. In 1878 the Argyll was refused its licence on the grounds that it was a "bawdy house". It then became a restaurant for four years after which it was turned into a music hall called the Trocadero. There were a number of other places that were called "night-houses", a peculiar Victorian institution which was a cross between a night-club and a brothel.

Another establishment, the Piccadilly Saloon, which stood where the London Pavilion now stands, did not really start its activities until midnight and continued until dawn. The dance saloons were living on the edge of the law and going to them brought with it an extra element of excitement. Men who would shun being picked up by a prostitute in the Haymarket would welcome the ambiguity and anonymity of the dance saloons. The prostitutes who plied their trade at these saloons could actually dance, many of them having graduated from opera theatres and music hall chorus lines to the dance saloons as it was a more lucrative career.

Assemblies

Between the dance saloons and the great ballrooms were the assemblies. One of the most popular was an assembly held three times a week during the season at the Cavendish Rooms in Mortimer Street. Assemblies were big business, sometimes catering for 2,000 people, and their organisation and ethos closely parallel ballroom dancing in the 1950s and 1960s. They were classless, sober and restrained, something that cannot be said of the open-air dances which went on in the Pleasure Gardens of Vauxhall and Cremorne which were more like the raves of the 1990s. After the death of Albert, when London became an altogether more sombre and puritanical place, the pressure from the middle classes eventually closed these assemblies down, as well as the dance saloons of the Haymarket, but at their peak they were part of a wealth of dance-related entertainment to be found in London.

17

Above: assemblies were big business, sometimes catering for 2,000 people.

The Ballet and Marie Taglioni

Victorian ballet was dominated by one person. She was called Marie Taglioni. She arrived in England in 1829 and for the next 20 years ballet held a revered place in London that it was never to hold again. Taglioni had put Paris in a frenzy in 1827 and she did the same thing when she arrived in London. She received £100 a night, a fortune, and both her father and her sister-in-law were employed to assist her at a time when serious music in England was held together on a shoestring budget. Taglioni married the Comte Gilbert Des Voisins in 1832, to whom she bore a son, but this did not detract from her popularity. In 1831 two other dancers, the Elssler sisters, came to London to challenge her supremacy The girls in the corps de ballet worked very hard but there was the bonus of attracting the young bucks of London. Many of them ended up marrying into the aristocracy. Fanny Elssler married the son of Napoleon and her sister Thérèse married Prince Adalbert of Prussia. One of the Bavarian dukes, Ludwig, married a Munich dancer 40 years his junior whose stage name was Lola Montez. She became the Comtesse De Lansfeldt. Because of these alliances there was always an eager supply of girls, prepared to endure the harsh working conditions, poverty and malnourishment associated with ballet training in the hope that they may win the heart of an aristocrat. However, when Fanny Elssler went to America in 1839 she made 179 appearances and was paid a total of £39,000, a huge sum even by today's standards. When she returned to England to dance before Queen Victoria the rivalry between her and Taglioni knew no bounds, each trying to outdo the other in stage gymnastics.

In 1840 a new rival appeared called Francesca Cerrito. Cerrito was the mistress of Michael Costa, conductor at the Opera House, who was said to be able to get through all Beethoven's nine symphonies in one evening and still leave time for supper. In 1842 he composed a ballet specially for Cerrito and called it *Alma*. That same year, after Cerrito's appearance in *Giselle*, a ballet especially written for her by Théophile Gautier and Adolphe Adam, a new ballerina called Carlotta Grisi took London by storm. By this time Taglioni and the Elssler sisters were well into their thirties whereas Grisi was still a teenager. Although she fell short on technical accomplishment due to her youth, she was nevertheless a ravishing beauty. In 1844 Grisi captivated London with her performance in a ballet called *La Perie* which was based on Victor

Above: Marie Taglioni.

18

Hugo's *The Hunchback of Notre Dame*. Following this, Grisi appeared in a ballet based on the Faust legend, playing Mephistopheles.

London was the cosmopolitan centre for ballet in Europe and, in order to appease the rivalry between the prima ballerinas a ballet was arranged featuring a pas-de-quatre in which Taglioni, Cerrito, Grisi and Lucille Grahn, the up-and-coming prima ballerina, danced together. It was written in such a way that they all had chance to showcase their individual genius. It was a huge hit as it climaxed with all four dancing together. It made international headlines across Europe and foreign courts received detailed accounts of it. Grove's *Dictionary of Music and Musicians* describes this dance as "one of the greatest triumphs of Terpsichorean Art on record".

There were, of course, other factors that made ballet so popular in early Victorian England. It fitted well with the romantic revival with its innocence and purity. The darkness of the Industrial Revolution was making nostalgia for the rural past fashionable. Simplicity was a quality that was lacking in the increasing speed of modern urban life. The fact that Queen Victoria, who was seen as being sweet and

virtuous, had replaced a long line of decadent Hanoverians was also a major factor. There was a belief that the new age would be one of delicacy and artistic endeavour. The upsurge of ballet in these 20 early Victorian years left an indelible mark on the history of ballet. The dress of classical ballet today is the same as it was in the 1830s.

The desire to emulate the pleasures of the upper classes induced the new music halls to take ballet from its lofty heights in the theatres and plant it on the stages of mass entertainment. It was the Alhambra music hall which led the way by promoting works such as *Die Fledermaus*, *Orpheus in the Underworld* and *The Bronze Horse* and, in doing so, made the tunes from these ballets popular. These ballet tunes, for example Schubert's *Rosamunde*, began to be included in the repertoire for military and brass bands as well as municipal orchestras.

19

Music of the Empire

Saloons

Victorian music hall as we know it was a direct development from the inns and taverns that existed during Shakespearean times. Popular music in early Victorian England was associated with good food and drink. Weekly singsongs were supplemented in the bars and saloons with professional entertainers and thus the tavern concert club was born. One of the most typical of these clubs was Evans's just off the piazza of Covent Garden. Down a steep stone staircase there was a supper room where one could get poached eggs on steak, devilled kidneys and red pepper and boiled potatoes in their jackets so that those who did not have access to domestic dinners could be catered for. Evans's was frequented by Charles Dickens, William Thackeray and the painter Landseer amongst others. There were no closing hours and it was strictly men only. The owner, Mr Evans, was a singer himself, noted for his renditions of 'The English Man' and 'If I Had A Thousand A Year'. This supper club established the tradition for singing as well as good eating and drinking. Our conception of popular music today is totally different to that of the Victorians. At these supper clubs the entertainment in the early part of the evening was devoted to glees and madrigals sung by choirboys from Westminster Abbey, St Paul's Cathedral and other churches. Even part of the mass or litany would sometimes be sung. At midnight the boys went home and a variety of singers took their places.

Look twice before you leap.

Charlotte Brontë (1816–55)

21   *Above: Victorian music hall as we know it was
a direct development from the inns and taverns
that existed during Shakespearean times.*

Behind the scenes the men were vulgar; it was only in front of ladies that there was any difference to their working-class counterparts. Coal-holes and cider cellars were a safety valve to counter the repressive puritanism of Victorian life. In these underground saloons the audience could escape from their public straitjacket and join in the choruses of ribald and obscene songs.

The audiences at these types of establishments consisted of fashionable and knowledgeable men who were quite happy to begin their evening listening to choirboys and then after midnight to sing bawdy songs at the top of their voices. They did not attend these places particularly for the music but for the food and drink and liberated atmosphere. They were, in effect, very informal gentlemen's clubs. With the coming of the railways, which made the entire nation more mobile, it became possible to visit London on cheap excursions. Guidebooks began to be published, listing all of these dubious clubs and soon the country gentry started patronising what were once exclusively city haunts.

The life of the song-and-supper singers was hazardous. The best of them managed the step up from saloon to music hall but for the rest, as soon as their audience tired of them, it was either the workhouse or becoming chairman of a music hall, dependent on the good will of the audience. They did not hesitate to hawk their songs from table to table for between half a crown and five shillings.

Eventually women were allowed into these men-only establishments and were permitted to watch the proceedings, although at first this was only through a grille. There were also the exciting "coal-holes" and "cider cellars" where almost anything went, and where songs of extreme obscenity and blasphemy were sung. It seems strange to us that, in places frequented by gentlemen, obscenities should have been encouraged but it must be remembered that in those days there were many coarse features throughout polite society.

In the inner suburbs, London was increasing in size and the population there also demanded entertainment. In 1838 the Grecian Saloon opened in the New Road area. It could seat 700 people, contained a church organ and epitomised the dream of the good life. It combined improvement with entertainment and introduced ballet to this new suburban audience. Between 1840 and

Above: the clientele did not attend these places particularly for the music but for the food and drink and liberated atmosphere.

1842 the Grecian Saloon produced over 20 operas. In 1841 the Britannia Tavern in Hoxton offered concerts, opera, vaudeville, ballet, dancing and farces. Tickets were six pence and a shilling and included refreshments.

> *That a man is successful who has*
> *lived well, laughed often,*
> *and loved much, who has gained the*
> *respect of the intelligent men and the*
> *love of children;*
> *who has filled his niche*
> *and accomplished his task;*
> *who leaves*
> *the world better than he found it,*
> *whether by an improved poppy,*
> *a perfect poem, or a rescued soul;*
> *who never lacked appreciation*
> *of earth's beauty or*
> *failed to express it; who looked for*
> *the best in others*
> *and gave the best he had.*
>
> *Robert Louis Stevenson (1850–94)*

Music Halls

The first real music hall opened in 1848 on Southwark Bridge Road and was called the Surrey Music Hall. In 1861 the Oxford Music Hall at the junction of Tottenham Court Road and Oxford Street opened. It was 94 feet long, 41 feet high and was lit by 28 brilliant crystal stars. It was deemed to be a "marvel of the age". The early music promoters sought to combine education and entertainment in the spirit of the Great Exhibition of 1851 and they formulated a policy of giving their audiences not so much what they wanted but what they thought they ought to have. Many of them even included art galleries in an attempt to bring culture to the masses.

The success of the Surrey and Oxford music halls led other owners of saloons and taverns to convert their own properties into music halls – the Mogul Saloon in Drury Lane was renamed the Middlesex Music Hall in 1851 and the Seven Tankards and Punch Bowl in Holborn became Weston's Music Hall in 1857.

Soon many music halls were being custom-built. Wilton's of Whitechapel opened in 1856, the South London Palace in 1860, the Bedford Camden Town in 1861, Deacons of Clerkenwell in 1861, Collins of Islington in 1862, the Royal Standard Music Hall in 1863 and the Metropolitan Music Hall in 1864. These were the golden days of music hall. In 1860 the Alhambra in Leicester Square, a magnificent Moorish structure,

had been designed "for every startling novelty which science and the fine arts can produce".

The success of these music halls in putting on wide-ranging programmes of entertainment, including ballet and opera, shows us how diverse the Victorian idea of popular music was. As far as the Victorians were concerned all music was popular music. However, the audiences were not as pleased with these "arty" entertainments as the music hall proprietors themselves and it soon became clear that some music was more popular than others.

The music halls that catered for the tastes of the audiences, rather than trying to improve those tastes, did better business and so gradually the music halls reverted to their original role of giving the public what it wanted.

Above: the success of the music halls in putting on wide-ranging programmes of entertainment, including ballet and opera, shows us how diverse the Victorian idea of popular music was.

24

The impression given by modern revivals of music hall is that the bulk of the programmes were made up of novelty turns – illusionists, slapstick comedy, gymnasts and ventriloquists – but this was not true in real Victorian music halls. It was singing itself that made up most of the evening's entertainment and the centrepiece of the show was the performance by the celebrity singer. These Victorian "pop stars" were relentlessly promoted, had carriages paid for by their management and were paid enormous salaries as well as other perks. So great was the demand for their services that they had to perform in several music halls a night. These singers were collectively called the Lions Comiques. Unfortunately, the smaller music halls were unable to pay the financial incentives that these singers demanded and so had to be content with a second string of performers who tried to copy the elite Lions Comiques. In 1878 a law was passed banning liquor from the body of the hall and so the link between food, drink and entertainment that had existed for decades was broken and the music hall went through another change. At this time, too, the stage began to be closed off from the audience with curtains. The smaller halls could not cope with the loss of revenue from selling alcohol and over 200 music halls closed throughout the country. Because of this, syndicates of halls began to spring up and chains of empires, palaces and hippodromes throughout the country began to appear. This intervention of big business ruined the intimacy of the old music hall in

the same way that music hall had ruined the bawdiness of the old saloons. In these new music halls the chairman, who acted as master of ceremonies, was abolished, tip-up seats were installed, ventilation, lighting and general comfort were improved and flamboyant schemes of decor were carried out resulting in a colourful vulgarity that was only paralleled by cinema decor in the 1920s and 1930s.

Music Hall Songs

The music hall song is difficult to categorise. There were thousands written, most of which have been forgotten. The best songs, however, were catchy and memorable and existed alongside simple ditties that were only sung a few times – a hybrid between the drawing-room ballad and the true music-hall song. In the early days of song-and-supper rooms the clientele was mainly middle class whilst the music halls catered for the whole social spectrum.

The most important difference, though, between the song-and-supper clubs and the music hall was the number of women in the audience. The three major divisions into which music-hall songs were split were current affairs and political commentary, romance and family and patriotic songs. There was a great deal of Cockney material for, although the audience was a mixture of classes including the nobility, the majority consisted of ordinary working people. The

Above: the best music hall songs were catchy and memorable and existed alongside simple ditties that were only sung a few times.

26

aim of the Lions Comiques was to weld this audience into one using the medium of the song. At first the audience observed but did not usually participate. The celebrity singers, however, changed this and worked upon their audiences with an instinctive skill, urging both those in the stalls and in the gallery to join in. The music hall was the setting for the "swell" who strutted about the stage and postured in his self importance. The audience had a love/hate relationship with the swell, both envying and disliking him.

The star singers of the Lions Comiques played on this ambivalent attitude by dressing as swells in their act. In this way they could both patronise and taunt their public. The Lions Comiques were not really swells, but were professional entertainers who had achieved their high status through sheer hard work.

Four artists stand out from the rest:.

Arthur Lloyd 1839-904

Arthur Lloyd's father was a Scots comedian and Lloyd was trained as an actor, moving from Glasgow to London in 1862. He wrote the words and music for many of his songs. Lloyd was a quiet and deep man off stage but had a vast repertoire of over two hundred songs of his own composition. His best-selling song 'Not for Joseph' sold over 80,000 copies of its sheet music. He was also very strong on nonsense songs like 'Chillingo-Wulabadorie'.

George Leybourne 1842-1884

George Leybourne, born as Joe Saunders, was an engine fitter from the Midlands. He came down to London and heard Lloyd sing and was inspired to become a comic singer himself. He made his debut at the Canterbury Music Hall and was soon earning £120 a week. He adopted the style of a swell and lived up to it but died in poor circumstances at the age of 42. He was tall, handsome, elegant and dressed in fur coats. His most famous song was 'Champagne Charlie'. This song was subsidised by the champagne shippers who paid him £20 a week and free champagne for endorsing their product.

27

Champagne Charlie

by Alfred Lee 1868

I've seen a deal of gaiety throughout my noisy life,

With all my grand accomplishments
I ne'er could get a wife.

The thing I most excel in is the
P. R. F. G. game,

A noise all night, in bed all day, and
swimming in Champagne.

Chorus:

For Champagne Charlie
is my name,

Good for any game at night,
my boys,

Champagne Charlie
is my name,

Good for any game at night, boys,
Who'll come and join me in a spree.

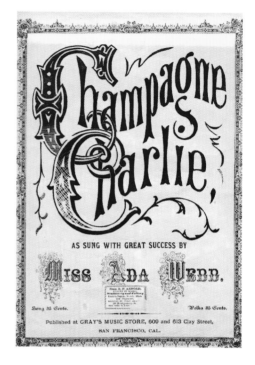

The way I gain'd my title's by a hobby which
I've got,

Of never letting others pay, however
long the shot.

Who ever drinks at my expense are
treated all the same,

From dukes and lords to cabmen down, I
make them drink Champagne.

Chorus:

From coffee and from supper rooms, from
Poplar to Pall Mall,

The girls on seeing me exclaim
"Oh! what a Champagne swell!"

The notion 'tis of ev'ry one,
if 'twere not for my name,

And causing so much to be drunk,
they'd never make Champagne.

Chorus:

Some epicures like Burgundy, Hock,
Claret, and Moselle,

But Moet's Vintage only satisfies this
Champagne swell.

What matter if to bed I go,
and head is muddled thick,

A bottle in the morning sets me right
then very quick.

Chorus:

Perhaps you fancy what I say is nothing
else but chaff,

And only done, like other songs, to merely
raise a laugh.

To prove that I am not in jest each man a
bottle of Cham

I'll stand fizz round – yes that I will,
and stand it – like a lamb.

Alfred Vance 1839-1888

Alfred Vance, also known as "The Great Vance", was a lawyer's clerk in Lincoln's Inn Fields before turning to acting on the provincial circuit. He was born in 1839 and his real name was Alfred Stevens. Before he became a music hall singer he had played Shakespeare in Manchester and had had a one-man show in which he had played 20 different parts. The Great Vance was the first music hall star to play the role of the swell.

G. H. McDermott 1845-1901

G. H. McDermott, born Gilbert Hastings Farrell, had a commanding presence and careful articulation. He was the master of the double entendre. He, too, had done an apprenticeship as an actor. He had been a bricklayer's labourer before entering the navy where he became involved in amateur theatricals. When he was eventually barred from the West End, because of his obscene ad-libbing, he retired and bought a string of music halls and prospered until his death in 1901.

The Lions Comiques were not only ballad singers but all-round entertainers. The spoken business between the verses was often as well rehearsed as the ad-libbing of today's television comedians. Style and deportment were just as important as the song. But these songs did not exist in a vacuum; they were an integral part of the music hall, along with the food and drink in the auditorium.

One can gain an idea of the music hall audience's interests by a study of the song titles. During the time of the Russo-Turkish war McDermott's song 'We Don't Want to Fight but, by Jingo, if We Do', written by G. W. Hunt, gave a new word to the English language, "jingoism", which appeared at the time of the Russo-Turkish War (1877–8). Disraeli, the prime minister at the time, ordered the Mediterranean fleet to Constantinople and almost precipitated England into the war by arousing popular feeling for the Turks, misleadingly identifying them as the victims being oppressed by the great Russian bear.

It seems that McDermott was in the pay of the Conservative Party and the arms dealers who were both interested in establishing involvement in that war. The Russophobes became known as Jingoes, and any belligerent patriotism has been labelled jingoism ever since.

Above: the Russo-Turkish war which inspired McDermott's song 'We Don't Want to Fight but, by Jingo, if We Do'.

'We Don't Want to Fight but, by Jingo, if We Do'

"We don't want to fight,
But, by Jingo, if we do,
We've got the ships,
We've got the men,
And got the money too.

We've fought the Bear before,
And while we're Britons true,
The Russians shall not
have Constantinople."

31

Above: Disraeli, British prime Minister
at the time of the Russo-Turkish War.

The music hall audience was acutely aware of contemporary events. There was a vast fund of feeling for the underdog and a clever singer could tap this at will. It was believed that Great Britain was the greatest and most civilised country in the world and therefore had carte blanche to meddle in the affairs of countries that were less fortunate.

In London, for instance, the music hall also appreciated the specific, in both locale and circumstance. In 1870 the Thames Embankment was opened and this event was good for a song – 'As I Strolled Along the Thames Embankment'. Belgravia, the custom-built suburb, inspired the song 'Belgravia' by Vance and also 'The Belle of Belgrave Square'. There was also 'Hampstead is the Place to Ruralise' and 'Hornsey Wood'. These local references reinforced the feeling of togetherness between the audience and singer which also bred the love of domestic songs. Unlike the love songs of the drawing room, the best music hall songs were wry, ironic, self-mocking and sentimental. For the majority of the music hall audience courtship was a short, bittersweet memory.

In dealing with love, marriage and courtship however, the singer knew that there was a line that must not be crossed. Homosexuality and perversions were taboo, particularly as the Queen would not approve, and could therefore only be subtly hinted at. Dynamic and assured as the Lions Comiques were, their songs were cold and calculating and even in their patriotic songs they inserted the occasional "er" and "um" to show that they themselves had reservations about the sentiments. It was only when women such as Marie Lloyd, Katie Lawrence and Betty Belwood came into the music hall that the innuendoes of the Lions Comiques were toned down.

Katie Lawrence became famous for her song 'Bicycle Made For Two' in 1892:
Other famous songs that are still popular to this day are 'The Daring Young Man on the Flying Trapeze', written to commemorate the trapeze artist Leotard, and 'Daddy Wouldn't Buy Me A Bow Wow' by Joseph Tabrar. Tabrar was an ex-boy chorister who wrote hundreds of throw-away songs in his 60-year career. He used to brag "Vagner!, Arthur Sullivan! – gertcher! – I can do all they could do and more, while you wait ... and on a bit of old paper the trotters is wrapped in!"

> "Daisy, Daisy, give me your answer do
> I'm half crazy all for the love of you.
> It won't be a stylish marriage.
> I can't afford a carriage.
> But you'll look sweet upon the seat
> Of a bicycle made for two"

33 *Above: the marrriage of Queen Victoria and Prince Albert in 1840. In dealing with love, marriage, the singer knew that there was a line that must not be crossed.*

'Daddy Wouldn't Buy Me A Bow Wow'

Josephh Tabrar 1892

I've got a little cat,
And I'm very fond of that,
But I'd rather have a bow-wow,
Wow, wow, wow, wow.

We used to have two tiny dogs,
Such pretty little dears!
But daddy sold 'em 'cause they used
To bite each other's ears.
I cried all day; at eight each night,
Papa sent me to bed.
When Ma came home and
wiped my eyes,
I cried again and said:

Refrain:

"I love my little cat, I do,
With soft, black silky hair.
It comes with me each day to school
And sits upon the chair.
When teacher says, "Why do you bring
That little pet of yours?"
I tell her that I bring my cat
Along with me because:

Refrain:

Daddy wouldn't buy me a bow-wow!
bow wow!

I'll be so glad when I get old,
To do just as I "likes".
I'll keep a parrot and at least
A half a dozen tykes.

And when I've got a tiny pet,
I'll kiss the little thing
Then put it in its little cot,
And unto it I'll sing …"

Other famous music hall stars were Dan Leno, Harry Champion, Gus Elen, Billy Williams and the aforementioned Marie Lloyd.

Dan Leno 1860-1904

Dan Leno was the most famous comedian of his generation. In 1883 he became a champion clog dancer. His first pantomime engagement was in 1888 and he is still remembered as the greatest of all the pantomine "dames". He performed relentlessly throughout England, gaining fans wherever he went. In 1901 he was commanded to appear before King Edward at Sandringham. He died in 1904 and crowds turned out three deep for over three miles to watch his funeral. His repertoire of songs included:

Going to the Races, Poppies, The Huntsman, Mrs Kelly, The Swimming Master, The Hard-boiled Egg and the Wasp, The Tower of London, The Grass Widower, The Mocking Bird, Who Does the House Belong to?, Clever Mr Green, The Mayday Fireman, My Wife's Relations, McGlochell's Men, Wait Till I'm His Father, The Shopwalker, Where Are You Going to, My Pretty Maid?, The Robin, Spiritualism.

Above: Dan Leno was the most famous comedian of his generation.
Above right: King Edward VII.

36

Harry Champion 1866-1942

Harry Champion was born as William Crump in Shoreditch, London. He made his first music hall appearance at the age of 15 using the name Will Conray. In 1888 he changed his stage name from Will Conray, and with his wide repertoire of songs, many of them sung at breakneck speed, became one of music hall's most successful artists. He worked into his seventies and died in London in January 1942. His repertoire included:

Any Old Iron, Boiled Beef and Carrots, You Don't Want to Keep on Showing It, Don't Do It Again Matilda, Ginger You're Barmy, Never Let Your Braces Dangle, Cover It Over Quick Jemima, I'm Henry The VIII, Let's Have a Basin of Soup, Standard Bread, You Ought to See The Missus in a Harem Skirt, I'm Getting Ready for my Mother-In-Law, The Old Dun Cow Caught Fire, I'm Proud of my Old Bald Head, Home Made Sausages, Ragtime Ragshop, I'm William the Conqueror, You Can't Help Laughing Can Yer? Little Bit of Cucumber, Doctor Shelley, Hey Diddle Diddle, Cockney Bill of London Town, I Enjoyed It, Everybody Knows Me in my Old Brown Hat, A Good Blow Out for Fourpence, The Old Red Lion, The End of my Old Cigar, Best that Money Can Buy.

Any Old Iron

Any old iron,
Any old iron,
An-y an-y an-y old iron.
You look neat,
Talk about a treat.
You look dapper
From your napper
To your feet.
Dressed in style,
Brand new tile,
And your father's old green tie on,
But I wouldn't give you tuppence
For your old watch chain.
Old iron, old iron.

Gus Elen 1862-1940

Gus Elen was born in 1862 in London. He was known as the greatest of the music hall "coster" comedians. The word "coster" comes from "costermonger" – a person who sells articles from a street barrow. He first started his musical career by busking on the streets before his first appearance in music hall as part of a minstrel duo.

He became more widely known when he decided to include in his act a number of Cockney songs. From 1891 onwards, he concentrated on characterisations of Cockney life, his performances on stage accurately capturing the accent and dress of this part of the London scene. His repertoire included:

Down the Road, The Coster's Pony, Wait Till the Work Comes Round, The New Pyjama Hat, The Publican, Pretty Little Villa Down at Barking, Nature's Made a Big Mistake, I'm Going to Settle Down, Dick Whittington, The Postman's 'Oliday, It's a Great Big Shame, 'Arf a Pint O' Ale, 'E Dunno Where 'E Are, The Coster's Muvver, The Golden Dustman, Mrs Carter, If it Wasn't for the Houses in Between

Billy Williams 1878-1915

Billy Williams was born Richard Banks in Australia. He publicised himself by travelling around London in an open car wearing a blue velvet suit, earning him the name of "The man in the Velvet Suit". His repertoire included:

Let's Have a Song Upon the Phonograph, I'm the Man that Buried Flanagan, It's Mine When You've Done With it, Land Where the Women Wear the Trousers, Poor Old England, Why Do You Think I Look So Gay? Save a Little One for Me, I Must Go Home Tonight, In the Land Where There Are No Girls, Don't Go Out With Him Tonight, When Father Papered the Parlour, A Tale of Paris, Soap and Water, All the Silver From the Silvery Moon, We Don't Want More Daylight, Little Willie's Woodbines, John Go and Put Your Trousers On, It's a Wonder What Little Things Lead To, As Good as Money in the Bank.

Marie Lloyd 1870-1922

Marie Lloyd became very famous for her – what were then deemed – "saucy" songs, especially her song 'A Little of What You Fancy'. The public knew her as "Our Marie". She recorded a number of songs towards the end of the Victorian era and amongst her repertoire are:

A Little of What You Fancy Does You Good, Something on his Mind, Every Little Movement has a Meaning of its Own, The Coster Girl in Paris, The Twiddly-wink, When I Take my Morning Promenade, The Piccadilly Trot, Put on Your Slippers, Woman's Opinion of Man, Revue, Now You've Got the Khaki On.

Unlike the performers, the writers of the late-Victorian music hall were poorly paid. If the songwriter was fortunate then a particular performer would buy the tune outright, for a guinea or two, and the writer would get a small percentage from the sale of the sheet music. In the 1840s and 1850s they usually charged 10 shillings a song or poems at the rate of five shillings for 20 lines and threepence a line thereafter. Many of the writers borrowed their tunes from old folk songs.

It might be supposed that with the larger theatres of the post-1878 period the audience would have great difficulty in hearing the words of a song because they were so far away from the stage without modern amplification technology. However, the empires, palaces and hippodromes had been designed with better acoustics than the earlier music halls which had really just been adapted from taverns, and once the law forbidding eating and drinking in the auditorium came into being this eliminated the clink of glasses, the clatter of plates and the chatter of the audience. To some historians of the music hall the great age runs from the 1880s to the start of World War I, but it still continued into the 1950s and a few survive even today, such as the Players Music Hall in London.

Burlesque

Burlesque became increasingly popular during Victorian times because it was the first time that women were seen on stage alone. Burlesques were send-ups of the stories they adapted and included straight acting, straight singing, dialogue, comedy routines and dancing and, although few of these pieces had lasting power, they prepared the ground for the Gilbert and Sullivan partnership and musical comedy in general.

At its best, burlesque was a music hall evening but with a plot. The writers of burlesque were mainly journalists and were fascinated by puns. Unlike the song-and-supper entertainments of the music hall the tendency of burlesque was towards the intellectual. In 1831, Eliza Vestris opened the newly decorated Olympic Theatre in Wych Street. This was the first time that a woman had controlled a theatre. Madam Vestris, a mezzo-soprano, commissioned J. R. Planché to write a series of entertainments such as *Olympic Revels* for which he was able to produce authentic classical costume.

Although music was an integral part of the burlesque, it was never considered superior to the words. Perhaps the most famous burlesque was *The Beggar's Opera* by Gay. Old tunes such as 'Cherry Ripe' were refurbished with new words. Bernand, the editor of *Punch* for 26 years, was celebrated as the writer of more than 120 pieces. His best-known burlesque was *Cox and Box* with music by Arthur Sullivan who was soon to be working with W. S. Gilbert.

E. L. Blanchard was known as "the hero of a hundred pantomimes", many of which are still being performed today – surprisingly, since the burlesque form was generally regarded as disposable.

The hundreds of burlesques that passed through the theatres gave the audience a taste for quick-witted dialogue. This was also being acquired by music hall audiences, newly attuned to the innuendoes of the Lions Comiques. It only needed someone to bring a sense of order into the chaos of burlesque and channel the work of the writers and bring in new players. John Hollinshead did precisely this. He took a lease on the Gaiety Theatre in The Strand and over the years produced 40 musical burlesques with a precision and deftness that had so often been missing. He achieved this in part by recruiting players from the music hall. He provided his patrons with a full evening of entertainment, knowing that his audience was basically middle class and wanted value for money. Hollinshead also paved the way for the Savoy Operas of Gilbert and Sullivan.

J. R. Planché 1796-1880

James Robinson Planché was born in 1796 in England. Like Gilbert's comic plays and operas, Planché's creations featured a strong emphasis on character development, a wealth of puns and musical parodies, all done with elegance and refinement. They also strongly featured topical humour, poking fun at everything from fashion to politics.

In all he authored 176 plays, operatic libretti and other theatrical entertainments, including numerous translations of foreign works. Among these were 23 melodramas, several comedies and farces, nine musical revues, 23 fairy-tale extravaganzas and nine burlesques of classical mythology. He also produced book-length scholarly studies of historical and literary material, including *The Conqueror and His Companions*, a book on William the Conqueror, along with a small review of English queens for Victoria's coronation. In addition, he wrote travelogues, children's books and magazine articles. He served for a time as the *Morning Herald*'s drama critic and was eventually, through his scholarly pursuits, appointed Somerset Herald. Sadly, owing to lack of copyright protection for writers, Planché spent much of his life in poverty. Along with Edward Bulwer-Lytton, Douglas Jerrold and others, he helped abolish the patent system of English theatre and extend the copyright to dramatic works in the United Kingdom.

His theatrical career, which lasted in the main from 1817 to 1856. provides an insight to the Regency and early Victorian stage in London. His memoirs, *Recollections and Reflections: A Professional Autobiography*, provided information about other notables of the time, too. His prose is highly readable and distinguished by his willingness to give credit to others and by his tendency to chatty anecdotes which give a feel for the personae of those involved.

During the final two years of his life, a group of admirers and friends helped him gather his collection *The Extravaganzas of J. R. Planché* featuring 41 plays and spread over five volumes.

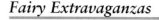

Fairy Extravaganzas

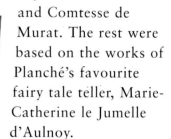

Extravaganzas are musical comic adaptations of the source tales, usually fairy tales.

Planché wrote 23 of these extravaganzas, six of which were based on the tales of Charles Perrault and one each on works by four other fairy writers, Charlotte-Rose de Caumont de la Force, Jeanne-Marie Leprince de Beaumont, Henriette-Julie de Castelau and Comtesse de Murat. The rest were based on the works of Planché's favourite fairy tale teller, Marie-Catherine le Jumelle d'Aulnoy.

It is important to remember that it was not until the late-Victorian period that fairy tales became associated with the nursery and children. The original French fairy tales were very sophisticated and witty, and Planché was fascinated by the works of such writers as d'Aulnoy and the other fairy romancers of France of the 18th century. His scholarship in translating

Above: it was not until the late-Victorian period that fairy tales became associated with the nursery and children.

collections of these tales, with endnotes regarding the historical background of their writing, is astounding. He searched out items as divergent as popular toys of the time and references to particular shopkeepers in d'Aulnoy's Paris. However, for the stage, the scholar had to make allowances for the showman. His extravaganzas featured astonishing special effects, amazing singing and dancing, and eye-catching costumes (which were all researched in his inimitable scholarly style). Still, his self-referential humour and his abundant topical references and puns provided much of the appeal.

Despite his love affair with the genre, Planché's first fairy extravaganza grew out of a need to vary his productions. By 1836, his classical pieces had grown so popular that other writers were copying his work, and he wanted to do something different. Eliza Vestris had grown accustomed to the success of the burlesques and so was hesitant to change. However, the writer's confidence was such that Vestris was persuaded that such a piece might work, and so Planché dusted off his translation of a French comedy he had witnessed while honeymooning in Paris 16 years earlier, *Riquet with the Tuft*.

43   *Above: the Brigand by J. R. Planché.*

Based on Perrault's tale *Riquet à la Houppe*, this adaptation by Charles-Augustin de Bassompierre Sewrin and Nicholas Brazier was comic but still suggested the tension and potential heartbreak of a good fairy story. Planché had long wished to write such a work for the English stage; prior to this, fairy tales were treated as vehicles for broad humour and for elaborate scenic effects, but not for a poignant dramatisation. He felt the plays could be much more effective if adapted in a way truer to their original spirit, allowing for both fun and more serious moments. Indeed *Riquet* was the only play he would adapt from another person's adaptation.

In 1837 his next fairy extravaganza, *Puss In Boots* was performed at the Olympic and was adapted especially for the Vestris-Mathews company. The character of Puss was very much in Mathews' accustomed line, as a wise-cracking and well-meaning assistant who fretted about his appearance; Vestris assumed a breeches role as the young man whom Puss befriends; and Bland was again a king. This piece established a pattern which future extravaganzas would follow, with Mathews always in a humorous part; Vestris in a part designed, in some fashion, to showcase her beauty and singing ability; and with Bland playing a pompous authority figure. In 1841 *Beauty and the Beast* was released at the Olympic with Mathews as a sarcastic clerk; Vestris played Beauty in a Versailles-inspired white dress with pink trim; and Bland was her father, a former Lord Mayor of London.

During the 1842–43 season his writing for the Vestris-Mathews ensemble was interrupted, briefly, when the company went to work for William Macready at the Drury Lane Theatre. There had been a dispute over contractual issues and Mathews and Vestris had walked out, although Bland and Planché remained. The play *Fortunio and His Seven Gifted Servants* (based on d'Aulnoy's *Belle-belle, ou le chevalier Fortuné*), was Planché's first extravaganza without his usual group. It was also the first in which Priscilla Horton acted, taking the title role of the young noblewoman who poses as a man to relieve her ailing father from military service. Similar to roles attempted by Vestris, it allowed Horton to dress in a typical "boy" costume with knee breeches, stockings, buckle shoes and a tight vest with loose sleeves – a parody of 18th-century men's costumes designed to show off the woman's figure. More importantly, it allowed Horton to showcase her fine voice and great emotional range. In the following years, she would act in many Planché works. With her refined sense of humour and pathos, some critics believed that she surpassed many of Vestris' own accomplishments. In addition, *Fortunio* allowed Macready and his colleague, Ellen Tree, another actress in Planché's best melodramas, to have input into the production of an extravaganza. Planché found that the tragedians actually had a very good instinct for how the work should be performed, with the right tension between passion and playfulness, and their coaching helped the actors to achieve the desired effect. Shortly afterward, Planché and Bland were reunited with Mathews and Vestris, but the input of the noted actors of tragedy and "serious" drama remained a valuable experience for Planché.

45 *Above: the character of Puss was very much in Mathews' accustomed line, as a wise-cracking and well-meaning assistant who fretted about his appearance.*

His art blossomed with the addition of Horton to the company, for she was an accomplished singer and a gifted mimic, whose breeches roles became amusing parodies of male behaviour, in contrast to the elegant sex appeal of Vestris' portrayals. At other times, her figure and musical prowess were more in demand. In *The Invisible Prince*, for example, Prince Leander, the hero, played by Horton, poses in classical draperies as a statue to observe Vestris' Amazon princess. The latter is dramatically forlorn, loving Leander from a portrait, owing to her fairy mother having forbidden her even to look upon mortal men. The princess's subjects sing to cheer up their princess who has told them of her passion for the stranger in the picture. After the Amazonian chorus, Leander comes to life and continues:

"I do believe you, sweet Princess,
And take you at your word;
I vow to make you happy,
And prove your ma absurd.
So don't mind that she-dragon,
My dear, my lovely bride,
But jump my gallant nag on,
And off with me ride.
Jump, jump my nag on,
And away with me ride. "

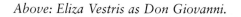

Above: Eliza Vestris as Don Giovanni.

The echo of the original words provides most of the humour; in the meanwhile, Horton's bell-like voice, accompanied by a harp, provided considerable musical enjoyment. Horton took some of her experience with extravaganza into her later career also when she helped launch the career of W. S. Gilbert.

Near the end of his career, Planché discovered Frederick Robson, and they worked together for three years. In 1854 Planché's *The Yellow Dwarf*, again performed at the Olympic and based on a tale of d'Aulnoy, allowed Robson to develop both the comic and tragic elements of the role of a freakish imp in love with a beautiful princess who shuns him. This eternal outsider amused audiences by absurd dances and songs, touched them with the poignancy of his hopeless love, and startled them with his wrath at rejection. Queen Victoria enjoyed Robson's acting enough to see the play several times.

Robson's next Planché role was as Prince Richcraft, a similarly skulking, malicious, but pathetic figure in *The Discreet Princess* or the *Three Glass Distaffs* based on *L'Adroite princesse*. His performance drew especial praise from William James (brother of Henry James), who remembered seeing it in his youth. In 1856 Robson gave his final Planché role, as Zephyr the air spirit, in *Young and Handsome* in which he performed well, but without the critical acclaim of the earlier roles. In this character, Robson also danced in the style of the prima ballerina Marie Taglioni. The role was entertaining, but seemed to remove Robson from his niche as a grotesque and unhappy man who becomes a villain because of rejection. It also led to the early collapse of the production, for Robson hurt his leg in the demanding dance and had to turn the role over to other performers, depriving the public of their much-loved star.

47

Opera of the Empire

G rand opera hardly existed during
Victorian times until the arrival of
Wagner's music. Even then it was
only attended by the upper classes and
aristocracy who mainly went to be seen.

However, one singer stands above all others
and was heaped with adulation. Her name
was Jenny Lind.

*You have no more right to consume happiness
without producing it than to consume wealth without producing it.*

George Bernard Shaw (1856–1950)

Above: Jenny Lind's invitation Polka.

Jenny Lind 1821-1887

Jenny Lind was born in Stockholm, Sweden, in 1821, the daughter of a language teacher. It is said that she was able to repeat a song that she had heard but once at the age of three. At the age of 10 she sang children's parts on the Stockholm stage. After turning 12, her upper notes lost their sweetness, and in her late teens she devoted her time to studying instrumental music and composition rather than singing.

At the end of this period her voice had recovered its power and purity and for a year and a half she was the star of the Stockholm opera. She then performed a series of concerts to obtain the means to go to Paris for further study, but the French teacher did not appreciate her talent and Lind returned to Stockholm.

At 23 years old, Jenny went to Dresden, and when Queen Victoria visited the city the following year she sang at the festivals held in the queen's honour. This opened the way to astonishing success in other German cities. In 1847 she went to London where she sang for the first time in concert and was enthusiastically received as the "World's Sweetest Singer".

In 1850, through the influence of P.T. Barnum, Lind visited America. Because of Barnum's amazing influence and power as an advertiser her tickets were sold for fabulous prices in New York, and she did not disappoint the wildest expectation. She subsequently married the Boston musician and conductor Mr Otto Goldschmidt. After her marriage, she appeared on the stage only at intervals and usually only at charity concerts. Indeed she became very much of a philanthropist.

In the last few years of her life, she again returned to London and lived there until her death in 1887.

Nowadays when English opera is talked about two names dominate the genre, namely Gilbert and Sullivan.

Above: Jenny Lind.

William Schwenck Gilbert 1836-1911

William Gilbert was born in London in 1836 and was the son of a retired naval surgeon. He had a pretty ordinary upbringing apart from an unusual episode when he was kidnapped in Italy, at the age of two, by a gang who demanded a ransom for his release. Beyond ordinary schooling, he took training as an artillery officer and was taught military science with hopes of participating in the Crimean War. He did not graduate until it was over, though, at which point he joined the militia and remained a member for 20 years.

After finishing his military training, Gilbert worked in a government bureau, a job which he hated. Upon receiving an inheritance from an aunt, Gilbert indulged his fancy and became a barrister. Called to the bar at the age of 28, Gilbert's law career lasted just a few years, however. Before leaving his law practice, he married the daughter of an army officer.

Gilbert had shown a talent for caustic sarcasm and wit from an early age and it was this talent that put him on the path to greatness. Starting in 1861, Gilbert contributed dramatic criticism and humorous verse to the popular British magazine *Fun*. Some of his work was accompanied by cartoons and sketches which he signed as "Bab". Many of the characters in the Gilbert and Sullivan operas were modelled upon some of Gilbert's "Bab" characters, and a collection of these "Bab Ballads" was later published in 1869.

The period from 1868 to 1875 was a very fruitful period for Gilbert, primarily because two plays which he wrote in 1871 netted him huge financial rewards. This was also the year that he collaborated briefly with a composer named Arthur Sullivan on a production entitled *Thespis*. Their collaboration spanned 25 years and produced a total of 14 comic operas of which *The Grand Duke*, the last, premiered in 1896.

Gilbert was knighted by Edward VII in 1907 and died in 1911, while attempting to save a drowning woman.

51

Above: William Schwenck Gilbert.

Sir Arthur Seymour Sullivan 1842-1900

Arthur Sullivan was born in Lambeth, London, in 1842 to a very musical family. His father was a bandmaster at the Royal Military College and, before the age of 10, Sullivan had mastered all of the wind instruments in his father's band. He composed his own anthem when he was eight years old. At age 14 he became the youngest participant to enter and win the competition for the first Mendelssohn Scholarship. He also won scholarships at several prominent academies and conservatories, the last of which was in Germany where Franz Liszt listened to his final thesis. At the age of 20 Sullivan returned to England, wrote the *Tempest* and became famous.

For the next 10 years he was a professor of music, a teacher, and an organist. Regarded as the leading composer of the day, he had many influential friends in every circle of society including many European monarchs. In addition to composing 'Onward Christian Soldiers', Sullivan also composed several major choral works, including *The Light of the World*, *The Martyr of Antioch*, *The Golden Legend*, and his only grand opera, *Ivanhoe*. Sullivan's first venture into comic opera was in 1867, with writer F.C. Brunand. Together they produced *Cox and Box* and *The Contrabandista*.

From 1872 onwards, he suffered from extremely painful kidney stones and it is said that his most beautiful music was composed while he endured great pain. He was knighted by Queen Victoria in 1883 and died in 1900.

The 14 Operas of Gilbert and Sullivan

Gilbert and Sullivan collaborated on 14 operas in the 25-year period from 1871 to 1896. These 14 operas constitute the most frequently performed series of operas in history. They are still being performed regularly throughout the English-speaking world.

The dates and performances shown are for their initial runs and are followed by a short synopsis:

Thespis, or The Gods Grown Old (26 December 1871; Gaiety Theatre; 64 performances)
The Gods on Mount Olympus are old and tired, so decide to take a holiday to earth while a group of travelling actors take their place. Most of the music for this opera has been lost, so it is played today only in re-constructions using either other Sullivan music, or original music. The general theme was used again in *The Grand Duke*.

Trial by Jury (25 March 1875; Royalty Theatre; 300 performances)

Hi-jinks in a courtroom, as the "bride" sues for breach of promise. This has only one act and is usually played along with another opera.

The Sorcerer (7 November 1877; Opera Comique; 178 performances)
With the help of a love philtre, everyone in the village falls in love but with the wrong person.

H.M.S. Pinafore, or The Lass That Loved a Sailor (28 May 1878; Opera Comique; 571 performances)
The captain's daughter and a common sailor aboard his ship fall in love. It became Gilbert and Sullivan's first smash hit.

The Pirates of Penzance, or The Slave of Duty (2 April 1880; Opera Comique; 363 performances)
A young pirate just out of his "indentures" falls in love with Mabel, Major General Stanley's ward, while the rest of the pirate crew want to marry the general's other wards.

Patience, or Bunthorne's Bride (23 April 1881; Opera Comique; 578 performances at both Opera Comique and Savoy Theatre)
The country women are in love with two poets while the poets are both in love with Patience, the village milkmaid. The brigade men do not see the point of aesthetics, but decide they had better give it a try to win the women's love.

53

Iolanthe, or The Peer and the Peri (25 November 1882; Savoy Theatre; 400 performances)

The Arcadian shepherd, Strephon, wants to marry Phyllis, a ward in chancery. Strephon, however, is half fairy but only down to the waist. His mother, Iolanthe, pleads his cause.

Princess Ida, or Castle Adamant (5 January 1884; Savoy Theatre; 246 performances)
Princess Ida decides that men are little more than monkeys in suits, so retreats to Castle Adamant to run a women's college. The men first infiltrate, then invade, the castle. This was Gilbert and Sullivan's only three-act opera.

The Mikado, or The Town of Titipu (14 March 1885; Savoy Theatre; 672 performances)
Set in Japan, Ko-Ko, a cheap tailor, becomes the Lord High Executioner for Titipu, while Pooh-Bah is Lord High Everything Else. Nanki-Poo, the Mikado's son, wants to marry Yum-Yum, Ko-Ko's ward. The situation gets complicated when Ko-Ko wants to execute Nanki-Poo.

Ruddigore, or The Witch's Curse (21 January 1887; Savoy Theatre; 288 performances)
None of the village girls stands a chance at marriage because all the village lads love Rose Maybud, but are too shy to court her.

Above: Advertisement for Princess Ida.

Robin Oakapple also loves Rose, but he becomes the wicked Baron of Ruddigore, and, accordingly, he must commit one major crime a day or die in agony. The ghosts of his ancestors step out from their portrait frames to confront him for not conscientiously carrying out this duty.

The Yeomen of the Guard (3 October 1888; Savoy Theatre; 423 performances)
Colonel Fairfax, sentenced to die in an hour on a false charge of sorcery, marries Elsie Maynard, a strolling singer, but he escapes, causing complications. At the end Elsie's boyfriend, Jack Point, dies of a broken heart. Or does he?

The Gondoliers, or The King of Barataria (7 December 1889; Savoy Theatre; 554 performances)
The King of Barataria is one out of two just-married gondoliers, but no one knows which one. As Barataria needs a king to put down unrest in the country, they both travel there to reign jointly, leaving their wives behind.

Utopia Limited, or The Flowers of Progress (7 October 1893; Savoy Theatre; 245 performances)
Having a rather idealistic view of England and the English people, King Paramount of the south sea island of Utopia decides that his people should adopt all English customs and mannerisms, and that his kingdom should become a "company limited".

The Grand Duke, or The Statutory Duel (7 March 1896; Savoy Theatre; 123 performances)
Ludwig, an actor, replaces Rudolph, the miserly Grand Duke of Pfennig Halbfennig, after "killing" Rudolph by drawing the ace in a statutory duel. By assuming all of Rudolph's obligations, he soon finds himself with far more wives, and prospective wives, than he knows what to do with.

When one door closes another door opens; but we often look so long and so regretfully upon the closed door, that we do not see the ones which open for us.

Alexander Graham Bell (1847–1922)

Plot Summary of Trial By Jury (25 March 1875 at the Royalty Theatre, London)

This was the result of Gilbert and Sullivan's first regular collaboration. Though called a "Dramatic Cantata", it is, in its perfect union of tuneful music and clever words, a direct forerunner of the more famous later successes of this inimitable pair. *Trial by Jury* is their only work entirely without spoken dialogue.

Characters
The Learned Judge, Baritone
Counsel For The Plaintiff, Tenor
The Defendant – Edwin, Tenor
Foreman Of The Jury, Bass
Usher, Baritone
The Plaintiff – Angelina, Soprano
Chorus of Jurymen,
Bridesmaids,
Barristers,
Attorneys

The Scene: A Court of Justice.

Curtain rises on Chorus of Barristers, Attorneys and Jurymen with Ushers.

The chorus, in their sturdy song, make known the course of events:
"For, today, in this arena,
Summoned by a stern subpoena,
Edwin – sued by Angelina –
Shortly will appear."

The Usher, having marshalled the Jurymen into the jury-box, gives them the judicial counsel to heed the plaintiff:

"The broken-hearted bride", and not "the ruffianly defendant", for,
From bias free, of every kind,
This trial must be tried."

The Defendant appears, asking "Is this the Court of the Exchequer?" and is greeted with scorn: "Monster, dread our damages!" The Defendant explains that happiness with the Plaintiff having palled, he became "another's love-sick boy". The Jury admit that once they were like that, but now they're respectable and have no sympathy with the defendant. The Usher orders silence at the approach of the Judge. The Chorus greet him with churchly song, "All hail, great Judge!"

The Judge, having thanked them proceeds to tell how he reached his exalted station. When young, he was an impecunious lawyer, "So, he fell in love with a rich attorney's elderly, ugly daughter."

The attorney turned plenty of cases over to him, and when he had grown "rich as the Gurneys'" he threw over the "elderly, ugly daughter". But now he's a Judge, "it was managed by a job", and ready to try this breach of promise case.

Then, at the Judge's order, the Usher swears in the Jury and summons the Plaintiff, Angelina. A chorus of Bridesmaids enters as her escort. While they are singing the Judge sends a "mash note" to the first Bridesmaid by the Usher, but when Angelina sings her graceful air he transfers his attention to her. He even admits that he never saw "so exquisitely fair a face"; and the Jurymen too profess great admiration for the Bridesmaids, then address the Defendant as "Monster". The Counsel for the Plaintiff makes his appeal to the Jury telling how the Defendant

57

Above: a Victorian court of justice.

"deceived a girl confiding, vows, et cetera, deriding.
And when the Plaintiff wished to name the day, he left her,
Doubly criminal to do so,
For the maid had bought her trousseau!"

Counsel and Jurymen join in singing to the Plaintiff "Cheer up!" while she sighs "Ah me!" in the style of Italian opera. The Plaintiff reels as if to faint and falls sobbing on the Foreman's breast, but when the Judge approaches she leans upon him instead. Edwin attempts to defend himself from their charge of "Monster!" saying,

"Of nature the laws I obey,
For nature is constantly changing.
and concludes by granting that
If it will appease her sorrow,
I'll marry this lady today,
And marry the other tomorrow!"

This seems reasonable to the Judge, but the Counsel, on referring to his books, finds that to marry two wives at a time is a serious offence, "Burglaree!". The Usher having restored silence in court, Angelina

proves her loss: crying "I love him", she embraces the Defendant, then adds:

"Oh, see what a blessing, what love and caressing
I've lost, and remember it, pray,
When you, I'm addressing, are busy assessing
The damages Edwin must pay."

The Defendant counters by saying that he is a bad lot, given to liquor, he's sure he would beat her and that she couldn't endure him very long; the Jury should remember this when assessing the damages. These conflicting statements are developed in a dramatic ensemble. The Judge therefore suggests that they make the Defendant "tipsy" and see if his assertions be true. To this proposition all save the Defendant object. Thereupon, the Judge is in a terrible rage for he is in a hurry to get away; he settles the case quickly by declaring that he'll

58

marry Angelina himself! And thus the "trial" ends in a mood of general rejoicing, while the Judge makes his concluding comment:

"Though homeward as you trudge,
You declare my law is fudge,
But of beauty I'm a judge.
To this all reply:
And a good judge, too!"

Most people can quote a line or two of W. S. Gilbert's verse or hum a few bars of Arthur Sullivan's music, but while many know the name of their entrepreneur, and may have heard he once quarrelled with Gilbert over a carpet, he remains a shadowy figure in the background. Little about his life or personality is known. Yet Richard D'Oyly Carte was a man of extraordinary vision and a talented musician whose business acumen set up a company which made him a richer man than his partners. On his death he left nearly a quarter of a million pounds, double the value of Gilbert's estate and quadruple that of Sullivan's.

Richard D'Oyly Carte 1844-1901

Richard D'Oyly Carte was born on 3 May 1844 in Greek Street, Soho, London. His father, Richard Carte, was a flautist and musical instrument manufacturer, a partner in the firm of Rudall, Carte and Co. The "D'Oyly", a Norman French name, came from his mother's side of the family, Eliza Jones. His maternal grandfather was a Welsh clergyman passionately devoted to art and literature and he did not approve of Richard Carte. Therefore Richard and Eliza were forced to elope and the couple's early married life was fraught with financial difficulties. However, their only son received a good education at University College School and he showed an early aptitude for music. He initially joined his father's business but, by the age of 25, had started his own theatrical and concert agency.

He also wrote operettas for The Royal Gallery of Illustrations, which he also conducted.

His agency prospered and he had an extensive list of famous clients, for whom he organised concert tours or speaking engagements. In 1874 he became the manager of Madam Selina Dolaro, lessee of the Royalty Theatre. In January 1875 a season of Offenbach's *La Péricole* opened at the theatre but to limited business. Victorian audiences expected a full evening for their entertainment so Carte decided that the Offenbach could be strengthened by the addition of a new afterpiece. He was separately acquainted with both Gilbert and Sullivan who, despite having collaborated on a Christmas show in 1871 and then produced a couple of drawing room ballads, seemed to have little in common.

By 1875 Gilbert was already staging his own dramatic works in a manner that was then considered fresh and natural. Sullivan seemed to be destined for a career in more serious music. He was hailed as the English Mendelssohn and, though he had dabbled with the odd lighter work, it was not thought to be where his future lay.

All this was to change when Gilbert ran into Carte one day in February. Carte asked if Gilbert could help him with a one-act piece and the librettist happened to have one to hand. It had begun life as a brief "Bab Ballad", but he had expanded it for the stage at the request of Carl Rosa, who planned to use it as a vehicle for his wife. When Madam Rosa died the planned production was cancelled. Carte immediately proposed Sullivan as a composer; less than a month later the "dramatic cantata", as it was billed, was ready. On 25 March the patrons of The Royalty enjoyed an evening which began with a comedy with the unlikely name of *Chryptoconchoidsymphonosomatica*, followed by *La Péricole*. The work was enthusiastically reviewed and remained a staple at the Royalty after its original companion piece finished its run.

Its success allowed Carte to realise something which had long been his dream – a school of English comic opera. He originally intended to commission a variety of librettists and composers, but such was the success of the Gilbert and Sullivan partnership, he had little time to encourage others. D'Oyly Carte enlisted four partners, three were in the music business and the last was a manufacturer of water carts. They took out a lease on the Opera Comique, and Carte announced the formation of The Comedy Opera Company. Gilbert and Sullivan obligingly wrote *Trial By Jury* which opened in November 1877. It returned a moderate profit and the directors of The Comedy Opera Company agreed to continue with a new work entitled *H.M.S. Pinafore* which opened in May 1878. That summer was unusually hot and initially audiences were uninterested. The other directors lost their nerve and put up closing notices several times. Finally Carte dissolved the partnership and took on the risk himself. Fortunately this was just as the box office experienced an upturn and soon *H.M.S. Pinafore* was the most successful show in town.

The other directors, annoyed at having lost out, decided that they still owned the sets and costumes and one night, during a performance, sent a heavy mob into the theatre to claim them. A pitched battle

behind the scenes followed, the stage hands of the Opera Comique winning. Later Carte won a further battle in court.

Carte then formed a partnership with his author and composer. Each contributed £1,000 and an agreement was drawn up in which Gilbert and Sullivan undertook to provide a new work as required on six months' notice. Their operas played not only in London but toured extensively throughout the British Isles, often with several companies running at once. These were billed as "Mr D'Oyly Carte's Company" until 1889, when the title The D'Oyly Carte Opera Company was introduced and so remained until 1961, when The D'Oyly Carte Opera Trust was formed. The operas proved equally popular in America and, to stop the numerous pirate productions, which paid no royalties to the authors, companies were sent out to tour there, too.

Above: the Victorian cast of a performance of HMS Pinafore.

Soon Carte had the idea of building his own home for English comic opera and bought a plot of land on which he built the Savoy Theatre. It was the most modern theatre of its time and the first in the world to be lit entirely by electricity. Much of the Victorian public had a fear of electricity, believing any contact with it would result in death. Carte made a rare appearance on the stage at the theatre's glittering gala opening on 10 November 1881 to reassure the audience.

He entered carrying a muslin-wrapped electric light globe, and then smashed it with a hammer. This caused the light to be extinguished, but Carte then held up the muslin to demonstrate that it was not even singed. The ovation he received eclipsed that given earlier to the cast. For the first time auditorium lights could be lowered during a performance and so lighting effects were introduced. Also, the room temperature was more comfortable than with the usual heat-producing gas lamps. Other innovations included the introduction of queues for the cheaper seating, a ban on tipping attendants and the provision of free programmes and cloakroom facilities. Of course, electricity was not then generally available. Carte used a patch of open ground adjacent to the theatre to house a steam-driven generator which produced 120 horsepower. In 1889 this open patch was used to further glorify the D'Oyly Carte empire when he opened the Savoy Hotel. This had taken five years to build, was the first building to be entirely fireproofed, had one telephone, two

"ascending rooms" (the first lifts in London) and 70 bathrooms, which caused the plumber to inquire if the expected guests were amphibious. Caesar Ritz was placed in charge of the restaurant and his chef, Escoffier, created Peach Melba for the distinguished Australian diva Dame Nellie Melba. Later a special suite of rooms was made available to Marconi for his experiments with wireless communications. The Savoy Hotel is now one of the most famous in the world.

Assisting Carte in his ventures from the beginning was a remarkable woman. Born Helen Cowper-Black, she was the daughter of a distinguished Scottish judicial figure. She took honours in four subjects at London University and then went on the stage, changing her name to Lenoir. Eventually she applied for the position of secretary to Carte and soon became an indispensable business manager. In 1888 she became his second wife in a ceremony at the ancient Savoy Chapel with Sullivan as best man.

Her supreme skills as a diplomat often smoothed out differences between her husband and his partners. It was not, however, sufficient to avert the biggest of their problems – the carpet quarrel. When the Savoy was built the partnership agreement was redrawn and contained the following clause:

"The said R. D'O.C agrees to pay each of them, the said W.S.G. and A.S., one third of the net profits earned by the representations after deducting all expenses and charges of producing the said operas and all the performances of the same, including such expenses as rental of £4,000 per annum for the Savoy Theatre and all rates, taxes, expenses of lighting repairs incidental to the performances and the rendering from time to time by ordinary wear and tear."

During the run of *The Gondoliers* Gilbert decided to query the accounts and was astounded at what he felt were higher than warranted production expenses. The figure that amazed him most was £140 for a new carpet for the Savoy foyer. He argued that it was not an expense "incidental to the performance" and that, at any rate, the clause referred to repairs, not replacements. His temper flared and after a major row he left and confidently contacted Sullivan, expecting his collaborator's backing. To his dismay Sullivan (who had little understanding of business affairs) took Carte's side and matters progressed to the point where Gilbert sued both his partners.

Above; the Foyer of the Savoy.

A close examination of the books revealed a discrepancy of some £1,400 which Carte was obliged to repay. This led to the partnership being dissolved with much bad feeling all round.

Sullivan's alliance with Carte was possibly influenced by the fact that Carte was at that time engaged in building a new theatre expressly to house Sullivan's first, and only, grand opera. Having succeeded in his desire to promote English comic opera, Carte now felt that he could do the same with English grand opera and commissioned Sullivan to write what he hoped would be the first of a new school. On land purchased in Shaftesbury Avenue the Royal English Opera House was erected and *Ivanhoe* made a triumphant debut. It soon became obvious that this would not receive the same public favour as Sullivan's works with Gilbert and that no further operatic works would be forthcoming. Within a couple of years Carte acknowledged his failure and sold the theatre, which then became a music hall.

The quarrel was eventually patched up and two more Gilbert and Sullivan collaborations were produced, but for the most part the Savoy housed Gilbert and Sullivan revivals or original productions either by Sullivan without Gilbert or by a variety of other authors (including one written by J.M. Barrie and Arthur Conan Doyle), but none was a spectacular success. At the end of the 1890s Carte's health deteriorated and he was not told in November 1900 of the death of Sullivan. Nevertheless, some days later he was found slumped by the window of his bedroom. "I have just seen the last of my old friend, Sullivan" he said as they helped him back to bed, referring to the state funeral of the composer which had processed past his home. Six months later Richard D'Oyly Carte died.

Carte's wife Helen, then assumed management of the opera companies herself. Although still doing good business in the provinces, the operas had lost popularity in London. Helen D'Oyly Carte made the bold decision to mount a repertory season of four operas in 1907. Up till then the works had been revived singly, but Helen persuaded the recently knighted Sir William Gilbert to supervise the productions. They were a tremendous success, despite *The Mikado* being dropped in lieu of a visit by a member of the Japanese royal family.

After Helen's death in 1913 her stepson Rupert D'Oyly Carte became chairman of both the opera company and the hotel group. For a time Victoriana was old hat and interest in the operas faded. But in 1919 Rupert brought the touring company (another innovation, a special London company had always been cast before) into the Princes Theatre for 18 weeks in a tremendously successful season that placed the operas at the heart of British theatrical life for the next 40 years. Rupert remained at the helm until 1948, when he died. Stewardship of the operas fell to his daughter, Bridget.

When the copyright of the operas ran out in 1961 Miss Carte formed The D'Oyly Carte Opera Trust to administer the operation of the company, though she remained the chairman of directors, living in a suite in the Savoy Hotel. In 1975 the centenary of *Trial By Jury* was celebrated by a two-week season at the Savoy Theatre in which each of the operas was presented in chronological order to an ecstatic series of audiences made up of Gilbert and Sullivan fans from around the world. Miss Carte was made a Dame of the British Empire in honour of the occasion.

Unfortunately, even in the midst of the celebrations, the future of the company was in doubt. Rising costs had taken their toll and standards were falling. Finally it was decided that the company that had been founded by Richard D'Oyly Carte a hundred years earlier could no longer be sustained and, at the end of a well-attended London season, the curtain was rung down on 27 February 1982. An encore awaited, however.

When Dame Bridget died a few years later she left money to the D'Oyly Carte Trust to reform the company. The New D'Oyly Carte was constituted not to operate continuously throughout the country, but to mount short seasons of fresh productions in London and major regional centres and they continue to this day, still with productions at the Savoy Theatre.

'Tis better to have loved and lost Than never to have loved at all.

Alfred, Lord Tennyson (1809–92), In Memoriam, 1850, line 27, stanza 4

Above: advertisement for the Savoy Theatre, under the stewardship of Bridget D'Oyly Carte.

Homes of the Empire

Home, Sweet Home

Music by Henry R Bishop 1823
Words by John H. Payne

'Mid pleasures and palaces though we may roam
Be it ever so humble, there's no place like home!
A charm from the skies seems to hallow us there
Which seek thro' the world is ne'er met elsewhere.

Home! Home!
Sweet, sweet home!
There's no place like home!
There's no place like home!

An exile from home splendour dazzles in vain.
Oh, give me my lowly thatch'd cottage again!
The birds singing gaily that came at my call
Give me them with the peace of mind dearer than all.

Home! Home!
Sweet, sweet home!
There's no place like home!
There's no place like home!

67   *Above: in Victorian England the piano was a*
status symbol for the lower middle classes.

Above: Queen Victoria and Prince Albert made music in the home more than respectable; It became a patriotic duty.

68

The Pianoforte

In Victorian England the piano was a status symbol for the lower middle classes. The piano had pride of place in much the same way that television does in every home today. All young ladies with pretensions to gentility were expected to have some musical accomplishment, whether they were the daughters of bank clerks or dukes. Queen Victoria herself had been taught piano by Mendelssohn and had a beautiful singing voice. The influence upon her maids-of-honour was considerable and it was a real honour for them to be summoned to accompany her on the piano. This, like all the other whimsies of Queen Victoria, passed down the social ladder.

Prince Albert himself was a music lover and the Queen went along with everything he did or believed and it was they who made music in the home more than respectable. It became a patriotic duty.

Felix Mendelssohn

Mendelssohn was born in 1809 into a wealthy Hamburg family. He studied the piano from an early age, under the tutelage of his mother. Later he received formal instruction from Carl Zelter in Berlin.

When still only a child, he began to compose chamber works. His family often held chamber soirées in their home, and young Mendelssohn had ample opportunity to hone his craft in these impromptu ensembles. Before long he was composing trios, quartets and operettas, and was making his mark as a pianist. At the age of 9 he made his public debut. By the time he was 17, his fame as a musical prodigy was spreading; that year, his first great composition – the overture to Shakespeare's *A Midsummer Night's Dream* – was produced.

In 1825 he wrote the brilliant *Octet for Strings* and revived the music of the Baroque master Johann Sebastian Bach.

69

Above: Felix Mendelssohn.

In 1839 Mendelssohn conducted a full-scale performance of Bach's crowning achievement, the *St Matthew Passion*. The performance was a great success, and it began a re-evaluation and appreciation of Bach's music that continues to this day.

Meanwhile, Mendelssohn began to forge a career of his own. In 1833 he was appointed Music Director of the town of Düsseldorf. Then in 1835 he was offered the conductor's post by Leipzig's legendary Gewandhaus Orchestra. By this point, he had already begun to write symphonies and produced more chamber works, and one of his piano concertos, as well as one magnificent oratorio, *St Paul* in 1836. His career development continued with a post at Berlin's Academy of the Arts and the origination of the Leipzig Conservatory in 1843. More works – the last symphonies, the *Violin Concerto*, the *Wedding March* – flowed from his pen before his health began to decline in 1846. Compounded by the death of his beloved sister, Mendelssohn's depression and decline deepened until the next year, when he died at the tender age of 38.

> *Why not seize the pleasure at once?*
> *How often is happiness destroyed*
> *by preparation, foolish preparation!*
>
> *Jane Austen (1775–1817)*

Piano Recitals

As the Queen invited the most famous musicians of the day to play before her and her family, so the aristocracy felt compelled to follow the Queen's lead and thereby set an example to their inferiors. However, drawing room music and piano recitals were not meant to be fun. The quality of music in drawing rooms ran the whole gamut from the abysmal to the superb. Even when there were professional musicians involved, drawing-room music could often be demanding and boring to the guests and it was often a test in endurance. These musical recitals were considered so important that music critics were invited and being present at these aristocratic recitals carried with it immense prestige.

In some of the great houses music was a ritual. At Belvoir Castle, the Duke of Bedford's residence, the summons for breakfast was carried out by the Duke's private band which marched round the castle playing sprightly music. The same procedure was carried out for dinner and, as soon as the dessert was placed on the table, singers came in to entertain the diners with songs.

Time lay heavy on the leisured classes and it needed a lot of filling. Music of whatever kind was worth having as a background to gossip and scandal. Some reluctant pianists or singers were pleased when the noise of the conversation obliterated their efforts. Most guests were, however, only too pleased to be asked to perform as amateurs all too often held high opinions of their own talents. Unfortunately for amateur musicians the talkative Victorians could rarely be kept quiet except in church. They were the definitive running commentators, whether they were the lower orders in the music hall where their participation was welcomed, the middle classes gathered in drawing rooms for music evenings or the upper classes at the opera.

The drawing-room ballad was the Victorian equivalent of today's instantly forgettable pop songs. Listeners believed they were getting good music, as did the composers and lyric writers, but often it was twee and overly sentimental using repetitive melodies. The three most prolific writers of Victorian drawing-room ballads were John Blockley, J. E. Carpenter and Fred Weatherley. Weatherley wrote over 50 volumes each containing 20 songs.

71

Above: even when there were professional musicians involved, drawing-room music could often be demanding and boring to the guests and it was often a test in endurance.

Lady Arthur Hill 1851-1944

Annie Fortescue Harrison was born in 1851. In her teens she wrote piano pieces which were mainly dance movements like 'The Elfin Waltzes' and 'Our Favourite Galop'.

She composed ballads and piano music as well as writing for the light musical stage. Her most famous song was 'In the Gloaming' which sold 140,000 copies between 1880 and 1889 and was still being printed in recent times. She married in 1877, but continued to publish songs and piano pieces.

Her operettas included *The Ferry Girl* and *The Lost Husband*. Other song titles were 'At Noontide', 'I want to Be a Soldier', 'In the Moonlight' (the sequel to her most famous song), 'Yesteryear' and 'Let Me Forget Thee'.

She died in 1944.

In the Gloaming

1877

In the gloaming, oh my darling,
When the lights are soft and low
And the quiet shadows falling,
Softly come and softly go.

When the trees are sobbing faintly
With a gentle unknown woe.
Will you think of me and love me
As you did once long ago?

In the gloaming, oh my darling,
Think not bitterly of me.
Though I passed away in silence,
Left you lonely, set you free.

For my heart was tossed with longing.
What had been could never be.
It was best to leave you thus dear,
Best for you and best for me.

In the gloaming, oh my darling,
When the lights are soft and low.
Will you think of me and love me
As you did once long ago?

The drawing-room ballad reflected the mood of its audience which wanted a buffer against reality. Financially secure it was yet full of anxiety about death, sex and the poor who were increasingly being stigmatised as the dangerous classes. Drawing-room ballads served not only to while away the long winter evenings but they were comforting in uncertain times.

Their overall tone may well have been melancholy, but it was rarely tragic. Sadness was always redeemed by a gleam of hope. The loved one might have gone but there was a good chance that he or she would reappear, either in the not-too-distant future or in the hereafter reflecting the Victorian interest in the spiritualist movement.

73   *Above: Drawing-room ballads served not only to while away the long winter evenings but they were comforting in uncertain times.*

The Tonic Sol-fa System

John Curwen was born in 1816. He had taught music to himself using the "Tonic Sol-fa" method of Sarah Glover, which utilised movable solmisation syllables as an aid to sight reading music from the staff. As a young congregational minister in his first pastorate, Curwen recognised the moral and religious value of hymn singing not only for his Sunday school children. His social ideals meant he believed that all classes and all ages of people should be able to learn music. Accordingly, he created and promoted an entire method of teaching based on this idea.

In 1841 Curwen was commissioned at a conference of Sunday school teachers to discover and promote the simplest way of teaching music for use in Sunday school singing. Curwen modified Glover's sol-fa notation and finally decided upon a pitch representation system which utilised the first letter (in lower case) of each of the solmisation tones (doh, ray, me fah, soh, lah, te) and a rhythmic notation system which utilised bar lines, half bar lines and semicolons prefixing strong beats, medium beats and weak beats respectively in each measure. For marking the subdivisions of beats he used a full stop for half divisions and a comma for quarter divisions, and for continuation of a tone from one beat to the next he employed a dash. As he originally conceived it, Curwen aimed to develop

74

music literacy in three successive phases: firstly reading from sol-fa notation, secondly reading from staff notation in conjunction with sol-fa notation and thirdly reading from staff notation alone.

He also made use of Glover's Sol-fa Ladder which he adapted into what he called The Tonic Sol-fa Modulator. Later still, Curwen incorporated French time names into his method and devised the pitch hand signs which, in a slightly modified form, are familiar to most contemporary music educators as part of the currently popular Kodály method.

At considerable expense to himself, he published his own writings, which included a journal entitled *Tonic Sol-fa Reporter and Magazine of Vocal Music for the People*. He also published textbooks and songbooks including *The Standard Course of Lessons on the Tonic Sol-fa Method of Teaching to Sing* which was first published in 1858. After 1864 he resigned his ministry and devoted most of his time to what had become a true movement in mass music education. Though Curwen did not truly invent tonic sol-fa, he developed a distinct method of applying it in music education, one that included both rhythm and pitch.

In Britain the growth of tonic sol-fa surpassed that of any other choral singing method during the nineteenth century. From its humble beginnings and an estimated 2,000 tonic sol-fa-ists in 1853, the movement was able to claim 315,000 followers by 1872 and to spread throughout the British Isles and to far outreaches of the British Empire including the Australian colonies, New Zealand, South Africa and Canada.

*Men judge us by the success
of our efforts.
God looks at the efforts themselves.*

Charlotte Brontë (1816–55)

It was also introduced by Victorian missionaries to their converts in India, Madagascar, Japan, China and the South Sea Islands. The method was even introduced into the USA.

In 1860 the tonic sol-fa system was officially recognised as a school music teaching method by the English education authorities in 1860, and by 1891 two-and-a-half million children in Britain were receiving instruction in tonic sol-fa in elementary schools. The tonic sol-fa method was also officially adopted by educational authorities overseas.

Two of the principle means that Curwen used to disseminate his Tonic Sol-fa method were firstly the Tonic Sol-fa College and secondly J. Curwen and Sons, Music Publishers. In 1879 the Tonic Sol-fa College was founded as the Tonic Sol-fa School in a building at Forest Gate on the east side of London. During its early years, the Tonic Sol-fa College instituted a system of certificate and diploma examinations. In 1944 the College moved to Queensborough Terrace, London, and took on the name the Curwen Memorial College. More recently the college was reconstituted as the Curwen Institute under the auspices of The John Curwen Society.

However, in the 1872 edition of *The Standard Course*, Curwen allowed the tonic sol-fa notation to exceed its former function as a mnemonic aid to sight singing from the staff and to become an end in itself. He decided to take the step of totally excluding the staff system of notation from the tonic sol-fa course, henceforth relying solely on his own notational system in the publication of textbooks, vocal music and even instrumental music. It was this isolation from the mainstream of music printed in staff notation which was to lead to the eventual decline of tonic sol-fa as a choral singing method. Nevertheless, it was not until after the turn of the century that any real indication of this decline was to become apparent.

John Curwen established the firm of J. Curwen and Sons, formerly known as the Tonic Sol-fa Agency, as the music publisher for the tonic sol-fa movement in 1863. Aside from its publication of music in tonic sol-fa notation and later in staff notation, in light of the decline of tonic sol-fa, J. Curwen and Sons were publishers of the tonic sol-fa journal under the successive titles of *The Tonic Sol-fa Reporter* and *The Musical Herald*. The firm then changed its name to the Curwen Press and continued up until the mid-1970s when it finally ceased operations.

Curwen died in 1880.

There is a great deal of unmapped country within us.

George Eliot (1819–80)

The Christmas Carol

The universal accessibility of popular carols has helped ensure their survival through centuries of historical turmoil, broad swings of fashion and even religious prohibition.

Originally carols were associated with dancing. The very word carol, traceable to ancient Greek drama, once meant to dance in a ring. However, since the frivolity of dance was frowned upon by the medieval church, as carols developed the old connection faded, though not completely. Today plenty of carols retain verses or titles that celebrate dancing as part of an appropriate manifestation of Christianity.

By the 14th century, carol singing was firmly established throughout Europe. In England the carol's popularity mirrored that of the narrative ballad. No amount of clerical complaining seemed able to stop the people from adding new carols and variants to the ever-increasing body of song and, since the tradition developed independently of the church at first, carol melodies grew out of popular folk song rather than ecclesiastic chant. Just as many sets of words could be attached to a single melody, lyrics could be paired with quite different regional tunes. The singable folk melodies and cyclic verse-chorus form remain to this day.

Carol singing was not originally limited to Christmas. New Year, Easter, saints' days and planting and harvesting times were among the holidays that generated their own carols. Some carols were general and could be sung all year round. The practice of carollers singing from door to door comes from the old "waits" tradition. The waits was originally a medieval town crier or timekeeper who sometimes played on a shawm or pipe and, in some places, bands of waits musicians sang and played in the streets.

The history of carol-singing in England has seen some dark times. After an explosion of popularity in the 16th century, when the first versions of many of today's carols were written, carols were among the cultural victims of the Puritans. The Puritan Parliament of 1647 officially abolished Christmas and other festivals altogether. Even though Christmas was again observed in England after Cromwell's demise, carols had to continue an underground existence for generations. Almost no new carols were published in England during the following 150 years. However, in the Victorian era all that changed.

79

Above: the Christmas Carol.

When Queen Victoria ascended the throne she had a strong desire to introduce a sense of seasonal morality at Christmas, with the emphasis placed on family values centred around the home. Although a movement had already started, the Queen's involvement helped change the face of Christmas from what had essentially become an austere event. In 1840, the Queen's consort, Prince Albert, had the idea to import a fir tree from his native country, Germany, where the Christmas tree was an old custom. From thereon, the candlelit, heavily decorated tree became an indispensable part of the Victorian Christmas festival. The popular press, including *Punch*, circulated pictures of the Royal Family gathered around the tree, and Victorian families identified strongly with the sober, close-knit image they portrayed. Soon the Victorians, with their love for nostalgia and grandeur, had revived many medieval Christmas customs and added some of their own, breathing life into traditions that survive today.

The revival of widespread popular interest in British carols is truly a Victorian phenomenon. When Victoria was born in 1819, carols were only being sung in a few isolated communities. Beginning in 1822, however, as collections of the old songs were published, the carolling tradition that had nearly died out was revitalised. The clergy all over England enthusiastically taught them to their parishioners.

The Victorian reinvention of Christmas was very much a family affair and, for those visiting relatives for the holidays, Christmas Eve meant an uncomfortable day of

Above: Prince Albert introduced the Christmas tree to Victorian England.

boughs. Candles were lit on the tree, and in Windsor Castle and a few other households children were given their presents on Christmas Eve.

In the run-up to Christmas, London was filled with the sound of music: from exotic bellringing and Italian bagpiping to the humble one-man-band. Groups of blizzard-blown carollers were often welcomed into candlelit, village homes for a glass of warming punch and a hot mince pie, reward for their vocal efforts in the spirit of Christmas.

On Christmas Day there were crackers to be pulled after the dinner was cleared away; games to be played; songs to be sung around the piano, such as Sir Henry Bishop's popular tune 'The Mistletoe Bough'; shows to be acted; dancing; and Victorian children were, for once, allowed to be seen and heard. Cordials or punch would then be served and, finally, Christmas would be over for another year.

travel on packed trains or horse-drawn coaches where valuable space was shared with baskets of game, presents and boxes of delicacies. Those awaiting their loved ones made last-minute preparations as the harmonious voices of wassailers floated on the crisp night air. Christmas hampers arrived and the butcher's boy made his last deliveries, passing the holly cart on the way selling door-to-door to those who couldn't get to the countryside to collect their own

Since being published and widely learned, the melodies to Victorian carols have become popular and recognisable even without the lyrics. The melodies have taken on lives and meanings of their own in our more secular society, but they still convey a sense of tradition and joy that seems in keeping with all that is best about Christmas.

81

Above: The Victorian reinvention of Christmas was very much a family affair.

The Most Popular Victorian Carols

'Silent Night' – dating back to 1818 when Pastor Joseph Mohr of St Nicholas Church in Oberndorf decided that he needed a carol for the Christmas Eve service and used a short poem he had written two years earlier. Franz Xavier Grüber, the church's organist and choir master wrote the tune. It became popular throughout Europe during the 1800s

'Jacob's Ladder' – popularised in 1871 via John Stainer's widely used "Christmas Carols New and Old"

'My Dancing Day' – collected in 1833 by Sandys and possibly dating back to before the 17th century.

The First Noel – believed to date back to the 1600s.

'The Wassail Song' – popularised by Stainer with many variant verses sung to the same melody and dating back to Elizabethan times, from Sandys' 1833 collection.

'The Cherry Tree Carol' – one of the most popular Victorian carols, this was sung to several melodies all over Britain.

'Righteous Joseph' – a Cornish nativity carol known to be have been sung as early as 1840.

'The Holly and the Ivy' – universally popular, with lyrics suggesting possible pagan pre-Christian origins.

'The Sussex Mummers' Carol' – dating from the late 1870s from Sussex.

'The Praise of Christmas' – collected in the mid-1800s by E. F. Rimbault, although the lyrics are at least 100 years older.

'God Rest Ye Merry, Gentlemen' – the most popular of all Christmas carols.

God Rest Ye Merry, Gentlemen

Thomas Bohlert

God rest ye merry, gentlemen,
Let nothing you dismay,
Remember Christ our Saviour
Was born on Christmas Day,
To save us all from Satan's power
When we were gone astray:

Oh tidings of comfort and joy

From God our heavenly father,
The blessed angel came,
And unto certain shepherds
Brought tidings of the same;
How that in Bethlehem was born
The Son of God by name:

Oh tidings of comfort and joy

Oh tidings of comfort and joy

"Fear not" then said the angel,
"Let nothing you affright
This day is born a Saviour
Of the pure virgin bright
To free all those who trust in him
From Satan's power and might":

Oh tidings of comfort and joy

And when they came to Bethlehem
Where our dear saviour lay,
They found him in a manger
Where oxen feed on hay;
His mother Mary kneeling down
Unto the Lord did pray:

Oh tidings of comfort and joy

Oh tidings of comfort and joy

God rest ye merry, gentlemen,
Let nothing you dismay,
Remember Christ our Saviour
Was born on Christmas Day,
To save us all from Satan's power
When we were gone astray.

83

Marvels of the Empire

The Great Exhibition

The events leading up to the Great Exhibition of 1851 were prompted by the success of the French Industrial Exposition of 1844. It was suggested to the English Government that it would be most advantageous to British industry to have a similar exhibition in London. However, the government showed no interest as, till then, few art or industry exhibitions had been more than local affairs.

Prince Albert was very much in favour of financing an Exhibition of All Nations himself but, even though this meant that the exchequer would have to pay no money, there was a lukewarm reception from Parliament. Albert's plan was for a great collection of works in art and industry, "for the purposes of exhibition, of competition and of encouragement", to be held in London in 1851. He said that it ...

> *"would afford a true test of the point of development at which the whole of mankind has arrived in this great task, and a new starting point from which all nations would be able to direct their further exertions".*

The government was persuaded to set up a Royal Commission which met for the first time in January 1850, and after digesting the concept that such an exhibition could make a profit it called for voluntary contributions nationwide. Prince Albert met with potential contributors from all over the country. Sir Robert Peel, the Archbishop of Canterbury, Lords Russell and Stanley, and the French ambassador were also present and the meeting was a great success.

The next stage was the setting-up of "The Commissioners for the Exhibition of 1851", and a total fund of £230,000 was raised. The size of the exhibition was set at 700,000 square feet – bigger than anything the French had ever managed – and the government was persuaded to treat it as a bonded warehouse, so that goods imported for the exhibition need not have import duties paid.

The commissioners set up a competition to design the building, and 233 architects sent in designs: 38 from abroad, 51 from around England, and 128 from London. The winner was a design by Joseph Paxton, who had struck on the idea of a simple repeating structure so that one cross-section could be repeated indefinitely to make a whole building. His original plan was modified to include a domed roof, so that some rather large trees on the site in Hyde Park could be accommodated without trimming them.

85   *Above: the opening of the Great Exhibition.*

The whole building was enormous – 1,848 feet long and 408 feet wide (with an extra annexe on one side 936 feet x 48 feet). The central transept was 72 feet wide and 108 feet high, and a grand avenue and upstairs galleries ran the whole length of the building. Altogether, 772,784 square feet (19 acres) were roofed over, not including the 217,100 square feet of galleries. This was an area six times that of St Paul's Cathedral. The total enclosed volume was 33 million cubic feet. Materials included 550 tons of wrought iron, 3,500 tons of cast iron, 900,000 square feet of glass and 600,000 feet of wooden planking to walk on. There were 202 miles of sash bars and 30 miles of gutters.

On 1 May, 1851 it was opened by Queen Victoria.

In its catalogue for the exhibition, the *Art Journal* wrote a glowing report:

> *"On entering the building for the first time, the eye is completely dazzled by the rich variety of hues which burst upon it on every side; and it is not until this partial bewilderment has subsided, that we are in a condition to appreciate as it deserves its real magnificence and the harmonious beauty of effect produced by the artistical arrangement of the glowing and varied hues which blaze along its grand and simple lines..."*

Above: Queen Victoria and Prince Albert at the Great Exhibition.

The catalogue continues: "Forming the centre of the entire building rises the gigantic fountain, the culminating point of view from every quarter of the building; whilst at the northern end the eye is relieved by the verdure of tropical plants and the lofty and overshadowing branches of forest trees ... the objects which first attract the eye are the sculptures, which are ranged on every side; some of them of colossal size and of unrivalled beauty...

"We have here the Indian Court, Africa, Canada, the West Indies, the Cape of Good Hope, the Medieval Court, and the English Sculpture Court ... Birmingham, the great British Furniture Court, Sheffield and its hardware, the woollen and mixed fabrics, shawls, flax, and linens, and printing and dyeing ... general hardware, brass and iron-work of all kinds, locks, grates ... agricultural machines and implements ... the mineral products of England ... the cotton fabric and ... In the British half are the silks and shawls, lace and embroideries, jewellery and clocks and watches, behind them military arms and models, chemicals, naval architecture,

philosophical instruments, civil engineering, musical instruments, anatomical models, glass chandeliers, china, cutlery, and animal and vegetable manufactures, china and pottery ... on the opposite side perfumery, toys, fishing materials, wax flowers, stained glass, British, French, Austrian, Belgian, Prussian, Bavarian and American products."

A total of six million people visited the Great Exhibition, and the costs were swiftly recovered as it was extraordinarily successful.

There were countless concerts and oratorios played throughout the duration of the Great Exhibition and many new instruments and musical inventions were displayed and played there. Amongst these were the guitarpa, a combination of harp and guitar, the 35-string violin cello and the saxophone. A number of mechanical and automatic instruments also made their debuts to the general public.

Mechanical Marvels

The invention of the phonograph and other sound reproduction machines started a new way of producing historical archives. Expressions of the human voice were no longer limited to their abstraction as words on the page, and the artistry and passion of  a musical performance could be preserved outside human memory. People could bring the sounds of the world into their homes, and a global culture began to arise out of the mixture of influences that a broad diversity of recordings could provide. Before radio and sound motion pictures, the phonograph and other "talking machines" reigned for several decades as the great modern innovation in audio culture and entertainment.

Ever since musical instruments were invented, people had attempted to turn them into self-playing instruments. It was not so much a delight in technical gadgetry, but rather people's desire for music which was the motivating force behind this development. As the centuries passed the demands made on the technical and musical capabilities of self-playing instruments increased steadily, and at the beginning of the 19th century "mechanical musicians" such as Johann Nepomuk Mälzel created whole self-playing orchestras, the "orchestrions".

At about the same time in Switzerland the musical-box was invented, consisting of a rotating brass barrel with pins which plucked the teeth of a sound-comb to create the sound. These became very popular in Victorian homes. Through the changes instigated by the Industrial Revolution it later became possible to manufacture devices more cheaply, thus making them accessible to everyone: the instruments called "Ariston" and "Herophon", which worked on the hurdy-gurdy principle and were controlled by perforated sheets of cardboard, sold in their hundreds of thousands. In 1890 the disc musical boxes, the best-known makes being "Polyphon", "Symphonion" and "Kalliope", took over.

Above: the "Symphonion" (left) and the "Polyphon" (right).

88

Automatic Musical Instruments

Automatic keyboard instruments and organs, typically of the barrel-and-pin variety, have a long history, although it was not until the Victorian era that they were accessible to the masses. In the early 19th century there was the barrel-and-pin London Street Piano, which later became popular in Italy. By 1825 Clementi & Collard had made a self-playing pianoforte, which combined a normal piano with "a horizontal cylinder similar to that of a barrel-organ, set into motion by a steel spring allowing it to play for 30 minutes before it needed rewinding and enabling it to play the most intricate and difficult compositions". The Cylindrichord was considered "an admirable and efficient substitute for a first-rate performer on the pianoforte... This instrument is extremely simple and differs altogether from the [pinned] barrel or self-playing pianoforte; it can be accommodated to the height or dimensions of any pianoforte, and when not in use for that purpose, forms a piece of elegant furniture."

Towards the end of the 19th century, the introduction of pneumatic techniques made it possible to manufacture self-playing pianos for the first time. The pedal-driven "Pianolas" and "Phonolas" took up residence in every respectable middle-class household. Electric pianos and giant pneumatic orchestrions were constructed for guest-houses and dance-halls, and a self-playing violin, hailed as the eighth wonder of the world, sent music-lovers into raptures. The hand-driven barrel organ, which was first invented around 1700, was developed further into a fairground and dance organ with a considerable volume of sound. Some of these can be seen in collections around the world today.

Above: the "Kalliope".

Shown at the 1851 Great Exhibition, the French Antiphonel, invented in 1846, was a key-top mechanical player that came in several forms.

The English organ pneumatic lever was adopted by Aristide Cavaillé-Coll in 1837. In the late 19th century pneumatic power was further developed to drive the keyboard or piano action and used perforated stiff cards with square or oblong holes according to the length of the notes to be played. The Autophon, using this principle, was invented in France in 1842. In 1846 a London patent was obtained for a "perforated note sheet" – the organ roll.

In 1863 the pianista was patented – it was an external "push-up" cabinet apparatus with a barrel, bellows and felted wooden levers or "fingers", powered by turning a handle. However, it had limited musicality as how quickly or slowly you turned the handle determined whether the music sounded either fast and loud or slow and quiet. In 1880 the first pneumatic self-playing piano, with a 39-note keyboard, was built. It was followed in 1882 by a 46-note "inner player" two years later, and the 65-note electrically-powered model in 1888.

A refinement of the pianista method came with the invention of the foot-treadled pneumatic Pianola in America, which was later pumped electrically. This took the form of an external "push-up" apparatus taken to any ordinary, unmodified piano keyboard. Later the mechanism was incorporated internally within the instrument. Pianola rolls were usually of the 44 or 65-note variety, with the full 88-note range introduced from 1908.

The Pianola was invented in 1896, by Votey of Detroit, USA, and initially took the form of a large wooden cabinet that stood in front of any ordinary piano. From the rear of the cabinet protruded a row of wooden fingers that were aligned with the keyboard of the piano and activated the

Above: The Autophon.

keys in the same manner as a human pianist. The player mechanism was powered entirely by suction, generated by pressing two foot pedals, while tiny perforations on small paper rolls represented the music. The "tracker bar", a pneumatic reading device over which the roll was transported, had a row of equally spaced holes; one for each note. A music roll perforation passing over the tracker bar caused a valve to open, which in turn triggered a pneumatic "motor". The latter operated a felt-covered wooden finger, pressing the corresponding note on the piano keyboard. The basic principle upon which Votey's system operated subsequently became the standard for virtually all roll-operated piano-playing systems. The Aeolian Corporation in the USA acquired the rights to the Pianola and marketed the very first instrument of its kind, later becoming the world's leading manufacturer of roll-operated instruments. The Victorians loved the Pianola.

Prior to the advent of the Pianola, various attempts had been made to devise a practical method for playing a piano automatically, although none of these achieved a notable degree of success in the home. Many of these early systems relied upon the use of a rotating wooden barrel with strategically placed pins to control the music, rather like a street piano. The musical repertoire was greatly limited, not least by the cost and dimensions of the wooden barrels, each of which would contain a small number of short tunes. In contrast, the paper music rolls used by the Pianola were cheap, compact and easy to mass-produce. Early instruments could only play a range of 58 or 65 notes from the music roll, whereas the piano typically had 85 or 88 keys. This prevented the accurate rendition of many classical pieces, some of which were specially adapted to accommodate the reduced musical scale. In addition, a number of manufacturers developed their own design of music roll, usually incompatible with other makes of instrument, an example being Hupfeld who introduced a 73-note system.

Sound Recording

The first successful sound recording device was developed by Leon Scott de Martinville in 1855. Scott's "phonautograph" used a mouthpiece horn and membrane fixed to a stylus that recorded sound waves on a rotating cylinder wrapped with smoke-blackened paper. There was no way at the time to play the sounds back, but the Frenchman's device was a crucial foundation for the developments that would come two decades later. Scott's phonautograph was manufactured and sold as a laboratory instrument for analysing sound, beginning in 1859.

Edison's Phonograph

In 1877 Thomas Edison designed the phonograph and directed John Kruesi, one of his top laboratory mechanics, to build a prototype. The device consisted of a cylindrical drum wrapped in tinfoil and mounted on a threaded axle. A mouthpiece attached to a diaphragm was connected to a stylus that etched vibrational patterns from a sound source on the rotating foil. For playback the mouthpiece was replaced with a "reproducer" that used a more sensitive diaphragm. Edison recited *Mary Had a Little Lamb* into the mouthpiece for the first demonstration. Even though he expected success he was startled to hear the "tinny" version of his own voice echo his performance.

That the invention of the "talking machine" was attributed to Edison was in part because of the publicity that attended his celebrity and the theatrical power of his demonstrations, and in part because previous inventions had earned him the means to have the device built. The first to conceive of a workable design had been the

Above: Thomas Edison in his laboratory, receiving the first phonogram from England.

Parisian Charles Cros, who delivered viable plans for a machine that would use discs to the French Académie des Sciences in April of 1877. This occurred several months before Edison came up with his own invention while working on a telegraphy device designed to record readable traces of a Morse code signal onto a disk.

In January of 1878, investors created the Edison Speaking Phonograph Company to oversee the manufacture and exhibition of the talking machines. Edison received $10,000 and periodic royalties. He continued to refine the tinfoil phonograph through mid-1878, feeding a popular enthusiasm for stage demonstrations of the "magic" machine which could imitate any language, cough, or animal sound that a sceptic from the audience could produce in an attempt to expose the "trick".

By October of the same year, however, Edison was coaxed away from the phonograph by an offer of substantial backing to pursue the invention of an electric light. As the novelty of the phonograph exhibitions waned, the audiences tapered off and the invention went through a dormant period nearly a decade long before it would transcend its status as a curiosity.

Genius is one percent inspiration and ninety-nine percent perspiration.

Thomas Alva Edison (1847–1931)

The Bell-Tainter Graphophone

The late 1870s and early 1880s were full of inventive breakthroughs and rapid advancements in communication technologies that came from a number of well-organised laboratories. Fast-shutter motion photography, the electric light, the telephone, and vast improvements in the telegraph were all developed within a few years of the phonograph. Alexander Graham Bell had invented the telephone in 1876, and Edison had become financially independent by designing a carbon transmitter for Bell's invention a few months before he began designing the phonograph.

While the two inventors' ability to inspire each other never yielded a particularly amicable partnership, it did fuel a competitive drive in both men that would entangle their lives for decades. The telephone won Bell the $10,000 Volta Prize from the French government, and he used it to establish a laboratory for experimenting with electrical acoustic devices. He gave his cousin, an engineer named Chichester Bell, and Charles Tainter, a scientist and instrument maker, the project of improving the phonograph. The Bell-Tainter "graphophone", released in 1887, displayed some key improvements to the Edison model. Cylinders were made entirely of wax instead of cardboard and tinfoil, which allowed for longer and more clearly defined recordings. The graphophone also used a loosely mounted "floating" stylus for clearer conversion into sound, and it resolved the pitch fluctuations associated with Edison's hand crank by using a foot treadle or an electric motor.

Above: Advertisement for a Columbia graphophone.

Berliner's Gramophone

While the cylinder machines were finally enjoying a period of wide public acceptance, a device that had already gone through several years of development was introduced to the US market.

Emile Berliner's gramophone, which used discs pressed in hard rubber instead of cylinders, was launched with minimal backing in 1893. The plan behind the first small-scale release was to attract more substantial backers by demonstrating the unique advantages of the gramophone. The discs were much cheaper to produce and any number of copies could be made from a zinc master. Berliner, who based his model on Scott's phonautograph and Cros's disc machine design, described the process this way:

"Gramophone: a talking machine wherein a sound is first traced into a fatty film covering a metal surface and which is then subjected to the action of an acid or etching fluid which eats the record into the metal. This record being a continuous wavy line of even depth is then rotated and not only vibrates the reproducing sound chamber but also propels the same by the hold its stylus retains in record groove. The original record can be duplicated ad infinitum by first making an electrotyped reverse or matrix and then pressing the latter into hard rubber, celluloid or similar material which is soft when warm and quite hard when cold."

Eclipsed by the cylinder machines' new heights of success, Berliner's gramophone was slow to attract attention. By 1896 Berliner's company had finally found some backers and was able to release the Baby Grand Gramophone, a spring-driven machine which could legitimately compete with the cylinder models.

With the advent of electricity all these machines would go through even more changes.

95

Above: a cylinder gramophone.

Concerts of the Empire

In 1838 the Lyceum Theatre put on the first British promenade concert. Entrance was a shilling and the theatre seats were boarded over so that the audience could stand. The 60-piece orchestra played overtures, waltzes, quadrilles and instrumental solos, and the concert was such a success it became a regular event. In 1839 further promenade concerts were held at the English Opera House, the Crown and Anchor Tavern, at Willis's Rooms, the Hanover Square Rooms and the Coliseum in Regent's Park. Normally, the musicians involved would only work during the opera season but the promenade concerts were so popular that full-time employment became possible. The top soloists and musicians of the day were also involved, resulting in extremely high standards. Philippe Musard, the Parisian founder of the promenade concert, also gave concerts.

Louis Jullien 1812-1860

Louis Jullien was born in 1812 in France, the son of a bandmaster. Unusually, he was given 36 Christian names after the 36 members of the Philharmonic Society, all of whom were his godfathers. He learnt to play many instruments as a child. He was a musician-showman of gigantic proportions and in 1840 the Drury Lane Theatre brought him over to give a series of summer promenade concerts under their French title "Concert d'été" with a 100-piece orchestra and 26 vocalists. There were floral and water displays in the auditorium to accompany the music and novelty effects designed to intrigue those attending such as cannon fire and performance on enormous, one-of-a-kind instruments. Such was their success that the concerts continued into the winter season with their multiple bands, choirs and soloists.

In 1841 the famous cornet player, Konig, the composer of the 'Post-Horn Gallop', the now military brass band standard, played at one of the concerts. A German opera season followed and then in the summer Jullien was back again at the theatre in Drury Lane. Admission prices were still kept within the reach of the general public and again the programme was a great success. Jullien composed his own quadrilles and waltzes especially for the promenade concerts. These

were published and sold in such volume that he started his own publishing and sheet-music business.

When he was not in London, he toured the provinces. As a showman he worked on a grandiose scale. He would conduct with a jewelled baton which was presented to him on a silver tray each night. Welsh quadrilles would be played using Welsh harps, English quadrilles with fifes and Scottish quadrilles with bagpipes. Part of Bellini's opera *Il Puritani* was scored for 20 each of cornets, trombones, trumpets, ophicieides and "serpents" (like French horns). Beethoven's *Fifth Symphony* was accompanied by four brass bands and Beethoven's *Violin Sonata* was performed by more than 60 players.

Jullien also embarked upon a number of monster concerts involving 400 musicians and three brass bands. He even had 20 nine-foot-long trumpets especially made in London in order to play a Roman march. Although the music critics hated these flamboyant extravaganzas, the general public loved them.

In 1851 he played concerts at the Great Exhibition, including one with five full pipe organs played simultaneously. Several new wind instruments by Adolphe Sax were also used by Jullien. Between 1853 and 1854 Jullien toured America, including performances in New York and Boston. He played over 1,200 pieces, bringing with him some of the top musicians of the day, and earned a great reputation for his concerts. Other promoters tried to emulate him, but without his level of success. In October 1854 he returned to London, performing the curiosity of what we know today as the "scratch" orchestra. In the "pantomime quadrille" the orchestra performed their duty of sneezing, snoring and laughing their way through but Mendelssohn, Mozart and Beethoven were still played, too.

In 1857 Jullien began to prepare for a universal musical tour to carry his music throughout the world, a very typical Victorian concept of civilising the "savages". However, he had been spending as much money as he had been earning in promoting a series of unpopular operas and he had to flee to Paris to avoid his creditors. He was immediately flung into a debtors' prison where he tried to commit suicide. He died in 1860.

Jullien's departure left a large gap in English musical life, but other musical entrepreneurs decided to carry on these promenade concerts using his same flamboyant methods. August Manns, musical director at

the Crystal Palace, was the first man to copy Jullien. Jullien's son came to London in 1863 to take up where his father left off, but he was a pale imitation and soon disappeared into obscurity. In 1873 the Covent Garden Theatre attempted to recapture some of Jullien's magic by employing big orchestras and military

bands, but these promenade concerts tended to be watered-down classical concerts and by 1893 the promenade seemed to be extinct. Then in 1895 the first charismatic conductor since Jullien appeared on the scene. He was called Henry J. Wood – the man to whom the modern promenade concerts at the Royal Albert Hall in London are dedicated. In the mid-1880s there were only a few concert halls in London suitable for promenades, including the Exeter Hall and the Hanover Square Hall. But then the piano manufacturers Chappell decided to build halls in order to promote their pianos. Chappell's St James's Hall began a series of Monday popular concerts called the Monday Pops.

Above: the Crystal Palace.

Oratorios

The oratorio is a form of religious music featuring a chorus, solo voices and instruments independent from the liturgy and on a larger scale than the cantata. It might seem strange to include religious music as popular music but Victorian tastes were eclectic. As in Jullien's promenade concerts, the oratorios gave their audiences large orchestras and large choirs which appealed to the Victorians' sense of grandeur. Oratorios took their themes particularly from the Old Testament. The appeal of the oratorio continued throughout the 19th century, as its public was stolid and conservative like the music and not given to fashionable whims. For the Victorian composer, to have written an oratorio was to have arrived. The oratorio was to the musician what the cathedral was to the architect. There was a belief that only the finest and the most moral of composers should write oratorios. However, the constant strain of writing in a religious style became difficult for most composers to sustain.

Above: the appeal of the oratorio continued throughout the 19th century, as its public was stolid and not given to fashionable whims.

Unquestionably the oratorio was a millstone around the neck of Victorian music because it was popular for the wrong reasons. Its acceptance as the supreme musical form in place of the symphony made many composers devote too much time and energy to its propagation, although it did ensure employment for choirs, singers and orchestral players. Professional musicians saw oratorio as their bread-and-butter music, but the quality of performance of an oratorio was usually deplorable. The music festivals were a great boon to these home-grown oratorios. The most famous was the Three Choirs Festival of Worcester, Gloucester and Hereford. There was also the Sons of the Clergy Festival, the Norwich Festival, the Birmingham Festival and the Cathedral Festivals of Durham, Ely, Peterborough and Salisbury.

Mediocrity knows nothing higher than itself; but talent instantly recognizes genius.

Arthur Conan Doyle (1859–1930), Complete Sherlock Holmes, Valley of Fear.

And I smiled to think God's greatness flowed around our incompleteness, Round our restlessness His rest.

Elizabeth Barrett Browning (1806–61), Rhyme of the Duchess.

In 1861, in York Minster, a festival of oratorio was held with 2,700 trained singers. When Sir Edward Elgar, who had been brought up on the traditions of the Three Choir Festivals, came to write his oratorio *The Dream of Gerontius* there was both a stage and an audience for it. Oratorio filled a need and it is to its credit that it gave employment to many talented people at a time when many composers had to work as church organists for meagre wages. It also helped keep alive the English choral tradition. It did, however, seem to make the English music lover believe that they were made more pure by being bored.

Sir Edward Elgar 1857-1934

Edward Elgar was born at Broadheath, near Worcester, on 2 June 1857. He had violin lessons in Worcester and London but was essentially self-taught, learning much in his father's music shop. From the age of 16 he worked locally as a violinist, organist, bassoonist, conductor and teacher, and also composed abundantly but most of his known work was written after he turned 40. His artistic struggles were compounded by the fact that he was a Catholic in a Protestant country and that he came from humble beginnings in a class-conscious society.

He first moved to London in 1889, with his wife Alice, but failed to garner any success. In 1891 he returned to Malvern where he began to make a reputation for his choral works. *The Black Knight*, *The Light of Life*, *King Olaf* and *Caractacus* were written within a specifically English tradition, but they were influenced also by the German music of Weber, Schumann, Brahms, Wagner and Mendelssohn. It was not until 1899, with his orchestral piece *Enigma Variations*, in which each variation portrays a different friend of Elgar's, that he realised his own style, taken further in his 1900 oratorio *The Dream of Gerontius*. Both the latter made him internationally famous.

His next works, *The Apostles* and *The Kingdom*, were two parts of an incomplete triptych of oratorios. Next a sequence of short orchestral pieces was followed by his long-awaited and much acclaimed *First Symphony*, swiftly joined by the *Violin Concerto* and *Second Symphony*.

In 1912 the Elgars moved to London again, but after the outbreak of war he achieved little besides the deeply reflective *Cello Concerto*. In 1920 his wife died and three years later he moved back to Worcestershire. There he completed the oratorio trilogy, wrote a *Third Symphony* and an opera. He also spent a great deal of time ensuring his works would be preserved by recording them for the gramophone. He died in 1934.

One of Elgar's most famous pieces is still played every year at the Royal Albert Hall's Promenade Concerts – his *Pomp and Circumstance March No. 1* of 1902. During World War I, it was combined with part of a poem by A. C. Benson (1862–1925) and was patriotically sung by the music hall star Marie Lloyd. It was immediately adopted and is the second most sung national song after 'God Save the King'. Perhaps the reason was that it can be sung with great gusto, and it shows the influence of the reign of Victoria.

Above: Sir Edward Elgar.

Land of Hope and Glory

Sir Edward Elgar 1902

Dear Land of Hope,
thy hope is crowned.
God make thee mightier yet!
On Sov'ran brows, beloved, renowned,
Once more thy crown is set.
Thine equal laws, by Freedom gained,
Have ruled thee well and long;
By Freedom gained, by Truth maintained,
Thine Empire shall be strong.

Land of Hope and Glory,
Mother of the Free,
How shall we extol thee,
who are born of thee?
Wider still and wider shall thy
bounds be set;
God, who made thee mighty,
make thee mightier yet.

Thy fame is ancient as the days,
As Ocean large and wide:
A pride that dares,
and heeds not praise,
A stern and silent pride:
Not that false joy that dreams content
With what our sires have won;
The blood a hero sire hath spent
Still nerves a hero son.

The other great patriotic song to come down to us from Victorian England was William Blake's poem Jerusalem. This was set to music by Sir Charles Parry.

Sir Charles Hubert Hastings Parry 1848-1918

Charles Parry was born in February 1848. Parry's early musical career at Eton and Oxford was fairly undistinguished, with a concentration of small-scale works such as songs, anthems and piano music in the style of Mendelssohn. In 1873, he began studies with the renowned pianist Edward Danreuther in London and it was only then that his individual style came to the fore. Danreuther, after studying with Moscheles and Hauptmann in Leipzig, returned to England to introduce the concertos of Chopin, Schumann, Grieg and Liszt. He combined these activities with instilling a veneration of the classics in his students and a keen personal interest in the newest music of Wagner and Brahms.

It was not until 1875 that Parry began to produce his major works. Although he had joined the Wagner Society in 1873, the chamber works he composed over the next few years showed the influence of Brahms in his approach. Through his association with Danreuther, he was presented with the opportunity of having his compositions played by some of the top musicians available in the chamber music recitals that were held at Danreuther's home.

In later years, Parry would go on to write in virtually every major musical form, including five symphonies, a piano concerto, an opera, a symphonic suite, an oratorio, and more than 30 works for chorus and orchestra. In 1893, he was appointed director of the Royal College of Music where he taught such future composers as Ralph Vaughan Williams and Gustav Holst. In 1898, he took on additional duties as Professor of Music at Oxford. He was endowed with a warm personal charm and this made him an influential teacher

In 1908, Parry suffered health problems, due primarily to the rigorous schedule he had taken on with his work at the Royal College and Oxford. On his doctor's advice, he resigned his post at Oxford and took a break by retiring to Sicily to regain his strength. After he had rested and recovered, in his last 10 years he produced some of his best works, including his last symphony *Symphonic Fantasia* and the symphonic poem 'From Death To Life'.

He died in 1918.

Above: Sir Charles Parry.

Jerusalem

Sir Charles Hubert Hastings Parry 1804

And did those feet in ancient time
Walk upon England's mountains green?
And was the Holy Lamb of God
On England's pleasant pastures seen?
And did the Countenance Divine
Shine forth upon our clouded hills?
And was Jerusalem builded here
Among these dark Satanic Mills.

Bring me my bow of burning gold!
Bring me my arrows of desire!
Bring me my spear!
O Clouds unfold!
Bring me my chariot of fire!
I will not cease from mental fight,
Nor shall my sword sleep in my hand
Till we have built Jerusalem
In England's green and pleasant land?

Streets of the Empire

Victorian London buzzed with the sound of outdoor music. In some back streets, away from the traffic, bands were playing all day long and these street entertainments carried on at night with groups of glee singers. The principal source of street music was mechanical – the barrel organ, the barrel piano and the hurdy-gurdy. Both the barrel piano and the barrel organ were operated by a revolving cylinder with teeth on it. Their tones were loud and coarse and they had a very limited repertoire. Their effect was somewhat like modern-day ice-cream vans. Sometimes monkeys, taken from the far reaches of the British Empire, cavorted about the barrel organs for the benefit of the customers. The Italians had the monopoly on barrel pianos and organs, since they had invented them; in London these were hired out from a centre in Clerkenwell.

The poorer members of Victorian society loved the organ-grinders as they would go into even the remotest slums and spread a kind of musical culture amongst what were considered the dregs of society. Their repertoire would include polkas, Christmas carols, music hall songs, sailors' hornpipes and waltzes. Although the selections offered were mixed, they all seemed to be reduced to a single tone level because of the simplicity of the mechanism and, although these instruments exert a certain charm today, at that time in London it was difficult to get away from them.

Above: sometimes monkeys, taken from the far reaches of the British Empire, cavorted about the barrel organs for the benefit of the customers.

Brass Bands

Throughout the Victorian age recreation grounds and parks were popular and in 1856 Sunday bands were permitted to play in these parks. Sunday for the working classes was a day of entertainment and music. There were religious taboos about enjoying oneself on Sunday and the Lord's Day Observance Society tried desperately to curb Sunday entertainment but to no avail.

The increasing interest in brass bands put many a Christian non-conformist into a quandary. The working classes crowded into these parks on Sundays to listen to military band music which was basically open-air music. They were primarily works bands, supported by employers.

107

Above: a Victorian park scene on a Sunday with entertainment by a military band.

Stalybridge Old Band was formed in 1814 in a private house adjoining the Hope and Anchor Pub, now the Fleece Inn, in Market Street, Stalybridge. The first members of the band, among others, were Thomas Avison, James France, and James Buckley. Its band room was in the attic of a shoe shop kept by Thomas Avison's father and, with a great deal of progress, more and more members joined up.

Its first public engagement was at the procession and foundation stone-laying of Chapel Street Sunday School but its most notorious engagement surely has to be the day it played at the Peterloo Massacre. As a favourite of Henry Hunt (Orator Hunt), the band was engaged to perform in support of him at a reform meeting to be held in St Peter's Fields, Manchester, in August 1819. Following their appearance, the band returned to George Leigh Street in Ancoats for refreshments but were disturbed by a supporter rushing in to tell them of the massacre of Hunt's radical supporters,

taking place at St Peter's Fields. The band members, fearing for their own safety, retreated out of the back door down a rickety ladder and through back streets, arriving hours later back at Ashton Moss. Following the events of August 1819, the band increased in popularity and its members were looked to as patriots who had suffered in defence of popular liberty.

The motive of employers supporting brass bands was not simply altruistic. After the 1832 Reform Bill had been passed there were many riots and large-scale civil disobediences and it was felt advisable, even prudent, to direct the attention of the workers towards more aesthetic pursuits. The movement of brass bands around the country in order to perform was greatly helped by the new railway system. Travelling expenses were usually paid by the company and most bands were members of the Temperance Society.

Competitions stopped brass bands from becoming stale but also helped individual band members get some idea of what the world was like outside their own towns. They also stimulated the mobility of labour between industrial cities and the manufacturing towns of the Midlands and the North. The patronage of employers helped to form a bridge between management and labour and it was noted that in areas where there were brass bands there were few strikes.

Brass bands had the edge over conventional orchestras in public performance because they were more suited to playing outdoors. Circuses, zoos, seaside resorts and parks all recognised this and capitalised upon it. It was fortunate that brass bands arrived on the musical scene when a repertoire was being created for them by the activities of Louis Jullien and his contemporaries at the promenade concerts. Brass band members attended Jullien's concerts and he introduced them to a range of works especially suited to their medium. These works came to form a major part of the repertoire of the bands.

Gradually brass bands became big business as the prizes were lucrative. With large sums of money changing hands, judges were sometimes accused of favouritism. The bandsmen also guarded their instruments with their lives in case they were tampered with. A magazine, *The Brass Band News*, was started in 1881 and the next two decades was the peak of the brass band movement. In 1888, at Belle Vue, 35 bands played to an audience of 8,000. In 1895 there were over 200 brass band contests throughout Britain, many of them offering large financial rewards and attended by an enthusiastic and knowledgeable fan base.

The versatility of the brass ensemble was also recognised by organisations such as the Salvation Army which began to use brass instruments in their street processions and to accompany their street corner proselytising. Indeed they even utilised a song by Arthur Sullivan:

Onward Christian Soldiers (Salvation Army march)

Music by Sir Arthur Sullivan 1871
Words by Sabine Baring-Gould

Onward, Christian Soldiers,
Marching as to war,
With the cross of Jesus,
Going on before!

Christ the royal Master,
Leads against the foe;
Forward into battle,
See His banners go!

Onward, Christian Soldiers,
Marching as to war,
With the cross of Jesus,
Going on before!

Like a mighty army
Moves the Church of God!
Brothers, we are treading
Where the saints have trod!
We are not divided,
All one body we,

One in hope and doctrine,
One in charity!

Onward, Christian Soldiers,
Marching as to war,
With the cross of Jesus,
Going on before!

Onward. then, ye people!
Join our happy throng!
Blend with ours your voices,
In the triumph song!
Glory, laud and honour,
Unto Christ the King,
This through countless ages,
Men and Angels sing.

Onward, Christian Soldiers,
Marching as to war,
With the cross of Jesus,
Going on before!

Military bands also offered entertainment of a similar kind at spas, watering places and park bandstands. Although their normal role was to accompany their troops into battle, they also had a secondary role of raising morale and recruiting. In 1860 there was a standing army of 100,000 men in Britain and most regiments had their own band. The band of the Royal Artillery and Grenadier Guards played promenade concerts themselves in 1871. Like the brass bands, the military band could also play out of doors and holidaymakers suffering from the British summer weather could relieve their boredom by listening to a military band playing on the bandstand near the beach in the same way that juke boxes would later relieve the ennui of modern youth.

110

The British Grenadiers

Thomas Augustine Arne

Some talk of Alexander, and some
    of Hercules,
Of Hector and Lysander, and such
    great names as these.
But of all the world's great heroes,
    There's none that can compare,
With a tow, row row row, row row row,
    To the British Grenadiers.

None of these ancient heroes ne'er
    saw a cannon ball,
Nor knew the force of powder to slay
    their foes with all,
But our brave boys do know it and
    banish all their fears.
Sing tow, row row row, row row row,
    For the British Grenadiers.

When e'er we are commanded to
    storm the palisades,
Our leaders march with fuses, and we
    with hand grenades;
We throw them from the glacis about
    the enemies' ears.
Sing tow, row row row, row row row,
    For the British Grenadiers.

And when the siege is over, we to the
    town repair.
The townsmen cry 'Hurrah, boys, here
    comes a Grenadier'.
Here come the Grenadiers, my boys,
    who know no doubts or fears.
Sing tow, row row row, row row row,
    For the British Grenadiers.

So let us fill a bumper, and drink a
    health to those,
Who carry caps and pouches, and wear
    the louped clothes.
May they and their commanders live
    happy all their years.
Sing tow, row row row, row row row,
    For the British Grenadiers.

One man, not an Englishman but a Belgian, had a huge impact on brass bands because of the musical instruments he invented. His name was Adolphe Sax.

Adolphe Sax 1814-1894

Adolph Sax was born in 1814 and was actually christened Antoine Sax, but seems to have been called Adolphe for most of his life. He was one of 11 children. His father Charles made clarinets, bassoons and brass instruments and was appointed "Instrument Maker to the Court of the Netherlands" by King William I from 1815 to 1820. Charles Sax was also awarded a prize from the 1820 Industrial Exhibition for his fine presentation of instruments. It was also Charles who pioneered research in the field of placing scientifically calculated holes along a length of tube to produce varying pitched notes. During most of this work he was assisted and observed by his son Adolphe. Adolphe began his formal education at the Royal School of Singing in Brussels. There he was also taught flute and clarinet.

It is thought that Charles concentrated his energies in the business of producing instruments to sell to make a living, while Adolphe experimented with new designs. Among the new experimental instruments to emerge were saxhorns and saxophones.

When Adolphe was 25 years old the lure of Paris beckoned. Whilst Sax was in Paris he met many notable musicians including Meyerbeer and Berlioz. However, he was eventually forced to move back to Brussels for economic reasons.

Above: Adolphe Sax's invention – the saxophone.

After a family tragedy in which Charles saw eight of his children die, both father and son worked together immersed in their work, to dull the pain of their bereavement. However, the Paris trip had had a lasting impact on Adolphe and he could not wait for the opportunity to return. He had several offers of work, some in London and St Petersburg, which he turned down. Finally, he was enticed to return to Paris by the offer of work for the French Military Service.

Almost immediately after his arrival in Paris, Sax started work on his family of keyed bugles: E-flat soprano, B-flat contralto, E-flat alto or tenor, B-flat baritone or bass with three valves and a B-flat with four valves. These were eventually to be known as saxhorns and were exhibited in 1844. The term saxhorn is one which has caused many an argument over the years because it implies that Sax invented the keyed bugle. Sax never claimed this, although he did state that his keyed bugles were of a much higher quality than the ones being manufactured by his contemporaries. It was the famous Distin family of virtuosi instrumentalists who claimed to have coined the name "saxhorn", to differentiate between the superior instruments manufactured by Sax and the existing faulty instruments of a similar type.

Having made these high-quality instruments the next goal for Sax was to publicise them and what better publicity could one have than a family of virtuoso players touring Europe playing his keyed bugles.

John Distin played in the Grenadier Guards as a key bugler. When he retired from the Guards he decided to embark on a solo career with his four sons, George, Henry, Theodore and William, all of whom were excellent exponents of the keyed bugle. After successfully touring the British Isles, John felt it was time to take his family to Europe and this is how, in Paris, he met Adolphe Sax. Sax was sent for by John Distin and they discussed Sax's new instruments. After suggesting a few modifications, Sax built a complete set of instruments for the Distins. The family played in Paris for several months and then returned to England at the end of 1844 where they were received as celebrities and the press followed them where ever they went.

The Distins playing Sax's instruments had a big influence on other ensembles around this time. Many bands in Yorkshire, Lancashire and Wales began to drop the woodwind instruments from their bands in favour of the more homogenous sound of Sax's brass. Blina Ironworks Band from Monmouthshire, and two bands famous today – Black Dyke Mills and Besses o' the Barn – all were influenced by the Distin 'Playing' advertisement.

113

Above: the superior saxhorn instrument.

Above: Adolphe Sax had a huge impact on brass bands because of the musical instruments he invented.

This collaboration between Sax and the Distin family was mutually profitable. The Distins became sole importers of Sax's instruments until they sold their company to Boosey and Hawkes in 1874. At this time Adolphe Sax was well established as an international instrument-maker. However, he went on to have many legal battles with other French manufacturers, some of which were very costly. He had many triumphs and some disasters along with many abortive attempts at inventing other instruments. He also suffered ill health in later life and in 1852 went bankrupt due to litigation against him. Sax, however, was a true survivor and, with the help of his friend Emperor Napoleon III, he re–built his business. He exhibited all over Europe but made his last visit to England in 1869. His many complicated financial disputes were becoming increasingly more disruptive to his business and he was continually in court protecting his patents or disputing others.

In 1873 he was made bankrupt again, and his only source of income was his post as Musical Director at the Opera. In December 1877 his famous collection of instruments was put up for sale to cover his legal costs and he also had to sell his printed catalogue containing over 467 drawings and prints. Throughout the 1880s Sax fought many lawsuits.

Adolphe Sax became a very bitter, disappointed and financially bereft man. A group of eminent composers of the day sent a petition to the Director of Arts telling him about Adolphe and his poor quality of life. A small pension was granted to him, which helped him in his last years.

Antoine Joseph, always known as Adolphe, Sax died on 4 February 1894.

Prejudices, it is well known,
are most difficult to eradicate from
the heart whose soil has never
been loosened or fertilized by education;
they grow there,
firm as weeds among stones.

Charlotte Brontë (1816–55)

115

Songs of the Empire

The Music Business

Victorian popular music was no different to modern popular music in terms of business. There were stars paid large salaries who were heavily promoted by theatre managements and music publishers sold vast quantities of sheet music which was the Victorian equivalent of the pop record. On the streets there were mini tycoons renting out barrel organs and selling sheet music to passers-by. Publishing houses promoted concerts and musical instrument-makers sponsored brass bands in order to publicise their instruments. It was not just musicians and management who profited. Popular writers such as Charles Dickens would give readings at concerts between the music, thus promoting their own works.

Although there was a great deal of money to be made in the Victorian music business, the composers themselves made the least compared with publishers, performers, managers and promoters. Opera was also a consistent money spinner for, although production costs were high, admission charges more than compensated.

It is a far, far better thing that I do,
than I have ever done;
it is a far, far better rest that I go to,
than I have ever known.

Charles Dickens, the end of A Tale of Two Cities.

Above: Charles Dickens would give readings at concerts between the music.

116

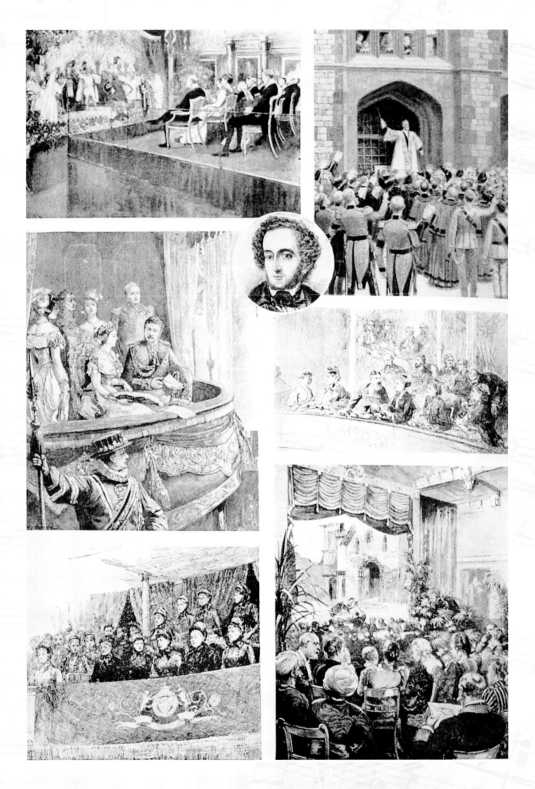

117 *Above: Victorian popular music was no different to modern popular music in terms of business.*

The field that was the widest open to money-making was the music hall itself. In 1878 there were 347 licensed halls and the managements vied with each other to get the top celebrities of the day. Managements were acutely aware of the value of advertising and in the West-End music halls hundreds of free seats were handed out to newspaper and magazine critics to review the shows. A number of magazines also sprang up dealing with music hall matters, many owned by music hall proprietors. In 1866 *The Magnet* was started and became the first magazine to run a professional directory of all the variety halls in the country. *The Music Hall Critic and Programme of Amusements* included interviews with celebrities but only lasted for seven weeks due to the intense competition of other publications, many of which also came and went in as short a period. Like theatres today, music halls were backed by "angels". No institution, with the exception of the cinema, enjoyed such a meteoric rise as the Victorian music hall.

While they were independent, music hall singers could be swayed by flattery. To many of them five pounds a week were riches indeed, particularly those who had risen from the working classes. However, management agencies soon began to appear to represent music hall artists – and to line their own pockets.

The comic singer Ambrose Maynard compiled a register of performers which could be submitted to managers. The performers paid a shilling for the privilege of being on the list and Maynard arranged gigs for many of the performers on his register. He would engage an artist for a fixed salary for a fixed period, make contracts with the managers for a higher fee and pocket the difference in the same way that young rock 'n' roll bands were exploited in the 1960s. Many of the agents also used their business to push their own music hall writing careers. Lesser artists began to resent the difference between their own salaries and those of the celebrities and so in 1870 the Music Hall Artists Association and Club was founded.

The injection of large quantities of money into music hall productions had mixed results. Soon, only shows that would produce massive profits would be invested in. The accent was on lavish productions that would have long runs. This resulted in large amounts of money being put into Gilbert and Sullivan projects and D'Oyly Carte productions which resulted in presentations superbly sung, accompanied and fitted out. Smaller productions became no longer viable.

Publishers who succeeded in reaching the drawing room audience, however, were sure of rich pickings and one of the most prolific of these was Chappell.

Chappell

In 1811 the Chappell company was founded by Samuel Chappell, Francis Tatton Latour and John Baptist Cramer. Cramer was one of the most fashionable pianist composers and taught pianoforte. One of the company's first publications was by Cramer, *Studies for the pianoforte*, which has had many editions since first published.

In 1812 Chappell targeted the nobility and gentry for sales of musical instruments. They opened a special room, called the Ware room, with pianofortes, cabinet pianos, squires and grands on display, which they advertised in local papers. The pianos were not at this time made by Chappell. However, they emphasised the fact that Messrs Cramer and Latour had personally

selected each of the instruments; this was a huge advantage over the rival retail outlets.

On 23 January 1811 the *Morning Chronicle* contained this advertisement:

"Chappell & Co beg leave to acquaint the nobility and gentry that they have taken the extensive premises lately occupied by Moulding & Co., 124 New Bond Street and have laid in a complete assortment of music of the best authors, ancient and modern, as well as a variety of instruments, consisting of grands and squires piano-fortes, harps for sale or hire."

Cramer suggested to the Chappells that they should invite as many of their professional friends and colleagues as was possible to form a musical society. The meeting took place at 124 New Bond Street in January 1813. This resulted in the formation of the Philharmonic Society which Chappell had close ties with for many decades.

CHAPPELL PIANOS

A New 50-Guinea Upright Grand

ON TERMS SIMILAR IN PLAN TO *The Times* "ENCYCLOPEDIA BRITANNICA."

35 MONTHLY PAYMENTS, EACH **£1 10s.**

50-GUINEA UPRIGHT GRAND.

Style IV – The action is perfect in touch and gives the performer every facility in producing gradations in tone from the most delicate pianissimo to the loudest sforzando. The sostenuto or tone-sustaining capacity is really surprising.

Liberal Discount for Cash.

CARRIAGE FREE IN LONDON.

ILLUSTRATED LISTS POST FREE. INSTRUMENTS SPECIALLY PREPARED FOR EXTREME CLIMATES. (Estd. 1908.)

CHAPPELL & CO., Ltd., Pianoforte Manufacturers, 50, New Bond St., LONDON.

Above: Advertisement for Chappell Pianos.

During the Society's first year of concerts Cramer and the old master Clementi took it in turns to conduct and play the pianoforte on alternate events.

In the early 1820s Chappell were awarded the Royal Warrant and in 1840 they started producing their own pianos. They opened a factory in Phoenix Street, Soho, but after a short time the popularity of their pianos grew so they had to move to new premises at Chalk Farm which has subsequently been enlarged on numerous occasions.

One of their nicest tributes came from Richard Strauss:

"Dear Sirs, I consider the tone of a remarkable sweet and sympathetic quality, and of musical sustaining power, the touch very responsive and light. Having always been used to pianos of German make, it was a great and agreeable surprise to me to find such a perfect instrument of English manufacture Yours Richard Strauss."

Samuel Chappell died in 1834 leaving behind his widow, Emily, and three sons William, Thomas and Arthur. Emily took control of the company. Although Thomas was working for Chappell it was not until 1840 that he became a partner in the company. Each of the sons did their part in running the company. In 1850 Thomas financed the building of St James Hall in Piccadilly. The hall opened in 1858 with a concert in aid of the Middlesex Hospital. Arthur directed the ballad concerts every Monday and Saturday which he ran for 40 years and they only stopped in 1926.

In 1895 Henry Wood conducted the promenade concerts alongside Chappell's ballad concerts. Edward Speyer and Henry Wood ran the proms until World War 1. Chappell terminated their contracts at that point and ran the proms until 1926 when the BBC took them over.

William Boosey, succeeded Thomas as managing director when Thomas died; William had worked with Thomas for many years, having joined the company in 1894. Boosey was responsible for introducing the royalty scheme as the only fair way to pay composers for their work. He also formed the Musical Defence League. Most of the music copyright legislation in the UK and overseas came about through pressure from Chappell.

In 1901 the Chappell Piano Co. Ltd was incorporated as a separate company from the music publishing side. In 1920 Louis Dreyfus acquired Chappell Music. Chappell still exists to the present day.

The Victorian Recording Industry

Whilst much of Victorian society regarded the phonograph as nothing more than a light amusement, Thomas Edison had renewed his interest in the phonograph and pursued extensive improvements of his own, most notably replacing the tinfoil sheath with a coating of wax and developing a battery-powered electric motor to drive the instrument. He was keen to advocate its scientific and more dignified use as an office dictation machine. Amid competing patents and corporate plans for the talking machines, and against Edison's protests, a market for their use arose again.

Something of a commercial recording industry had started up in 1890. Musicians would record on several phonographs at once, repeating their performance until enough cylinders were produced to satisfy demand. Wax was a poor medium for capturing music of any quality and the cylinders could only hold two minutes of music, but the entertainment value of having a wide variety of recordings to choose from made the new industry quite attractive, nonetheless.

Numerous "phonograph parlours" opened to exploit the invention's lucrative commercial possibilities. A customer could speak into a tube to request one of as many as 150 titles and listen to a recording played on the floor below that was piped into two ear horns at the customer's private desk.

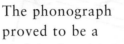

The phonograph parlours soon added individual coin-operated kinetoscopes that flipped photographs past a viewer, creating the first common motion picture illusions.

The phonograph proved to be a useful advertising medium. Machines that could be activated by the touch of a button were mounted in conspicuous places, in keeping with the message of an 1894 promotional statement: "Nobody will refuse to listen to a fine song or concert piece or oration, even if interrupted by the modest remark, 'Tartar's Baking Powder Is Best', or 'Wash The Baby With Pears Soap'."

It became clear that the phonograph was going to play a large part in the entertainment world. Thomas Macdonald, the manager of a graphophone factory, developed an inexpensive and reliable clockwork motor. This enabled the Bell-Tainter camp, now doing business as the Columbia Phonograph Company, to launch a fully fledged retail venture with a clockwork-driven machine which they called the "Graphophone Grand".

121   *Above: A Columbia gramophone advert.*

The Victorian Record Companies

There were three major selling agencies that would dominate the sale of gramophones for many years. These were the National Gramophone Company, which sold Berliner gramophones; the Columbia Phonograph Company, which sold Bell-Tainter graphophones; and the National Phonograph Company, which sold Edison phonographs. There were also corporations that held and manufactured under patent rights. Among these were Volta Graphophone, associated with Bell-Tainter machines, and the Victor Talking Machine Company, which was Berliner's partnership with Eldridge Johnson, the man who had developed the gramophone's spring drive.

The commercial success of the machines in the late 1890s sparked a number of corporate lawsuits and patent battles, and prompted several new technical innovations. The Berliner people developed a new disc-stamping process and Duranoid, a shellac-based plastic material that proved far superior to rubber. Edison's camp came up with a machine that could play two cylinders with one winding of the spring drive. An inventor named Harold Short developed a

compressed-air amplifier. Some odd new twists on turn-of-the century talking machines included an intriguing variety of handsome and, at times, bizarre cabinets and horns; a disc design that allowed for 12 minutes of play and moved the stylus outwards, from the centre; a method of linking the sound patterns to a mouthpiece so people could plug their ears and "listen with their teeth"; and novelty records made out of chocolate which could be eaten when they became too worn out to play.

Above: Advertisements for gramophones.

The Worldwide Recording Boom

The first gramophone records were sold in England in August 1898 and these were named "Berliners" after the main manufacturer. In the United States, executives of the Gramophone Company sought greater international influence. They sent a young musician and talent scout named Fred Gaisberg to the great cities of Europe and Asia with an elaborate and bulky assemblage of recording equipment. Gaisberg's tireless enthusiasm for recording all manner of church and military music, street and tavern acts, and folk performances provided an enormous variety of recordings the company could offer to gramophone enthusiasts.

Talking machines were enjoying a tremendous surge in popularity not only in Victorian England but across most of Europe near the turn of the century. It was easy to persuade local acts to record, but the Gramophone Company was presented with a formidable challenge when it sought to record Europe's great opera stars. Most of the singers scoffed at the idea of being associated with an amusement gadget, but a new wax-engraving process improved recording quality dramatically and by 1901 the Gramophone Company had made 60 records by four stars of the Russian Imperial Opera. This coup prompted Gaisberg to pursue the great young tenor, Caruso, which he did successfully.

The major record labels in England at this time were Edison Bell, Britannic, Duophone, Empire and Zonophone.

Many music hall artists, ballad singers, concert pianists and orchestras recorded their music for posterity at the close of the Victorian era. Thankfully many are preserved to this day.

Above: Advertisement for a recording of Caruso.

Epilogue

In 1901 Queen Victoria died. A new century and era began and with it came new music, yet the legacy of Victorian music lives on today.

Rule, Britannia

James Thomson 1740

When Britain first, at heaven's command,
  Arose from out the azure main,
  This was the charter of the land,
  And guardian angels sung this strain:

  Rule, Britannia, rule the waves;
    Britons never will be slaves.

  The nations, not so blest as thee,
  Must, in their turns, to tyrants fall,
While thou shalt flourish great and free,
  The dread and envy of them all.

  Still more majestic shalt thou rise,
More dreadful, from each foreign stroke,
  As the loud blast that tears the skies,
  Serves but to root thy native oak.

  Thee haughty tyrants ne'er shall tame:
  All their attempts to bend thee down,
  Will but arouse thy generous flame;
  But work their woe, and thy renown.

  To thee belongs the rural reign;
  Thy cities shall with commerce shine;
  All thine shall be the subject main;
  And every shore it circles thine.

  The Muses, still with freedom found,
    Shall to thy happy coast repair.
  Blest isle! With matchless beauty crowned,
  And manly hearts to guard the fair.

125

Index

128